NOTES

ON THE

BATTLE OF JENA,

14th OCTOBER, 1806.

BY

AN OFFICER OF THE R. STAFF CORPS,

(LATE OF THE ROYAL ARTILLERY.)

ILLUSTRATED BY ENGRAVINGS.

The Naval & Military Press Ltd

published in association with

FIREPOWER
The Royal Artillery Museum
Woolwich

Published by
The Naval & Military Press Ltd
Unit 10 Ridgewood Industrial Park,
Uckfield, East Sussex,
TN22 5QE England
Tel: +44 (0) 1825 749494
Fax: +44 (0) 1825 765701
www.naval-military-press.com

in association with

**FIREPOWER
The Royal Artillery Museum, Woolwich**
www.firepower.org.uk

In reprinting in facsimile from the original, any imperfections are inevitably reproduced and the quality may fall short of modern type and cartographic standards.

PREFATORY NOTE.

The Author regrets that he was prevented by circumstances from correcting the proof-sheets himself, in consequence of which the following errors of the press require to be marked out by the reader.

Page 13, line 6, for "*Neinungen,*" read "*Meinungen.*"
15, last line, for "*Königshofeu,*" read "*Konigshofen.*"
24, line 7, for "*Pölnitz,*" read "*Pölnitz.*"
same page, line 3 from bottom,   do.
28, last line, for "*Salin,*" read "*Salm.*"
37, line 7 from bottom, for "*Stobsa,*" read "*Stobru.*"
38, line 8 from bottom, for "*Nühlthal,*" read "*Mühlthal.*"
46, line 8, for "*Lancha,*" read "*Laucha.*"
49, line 9, for "*Gudiu,*" read "*Gudin.*"
85, line 15, for "*Hendelet,*" read "*Heudelet.*"

DIRECTIONS FOR THE PLATES.

Plate A, at the commencement, on the *left* hand side.
Plate B, after the Introduction, on the *left* hand side.
The large Plate at the end, on the *right* hand.

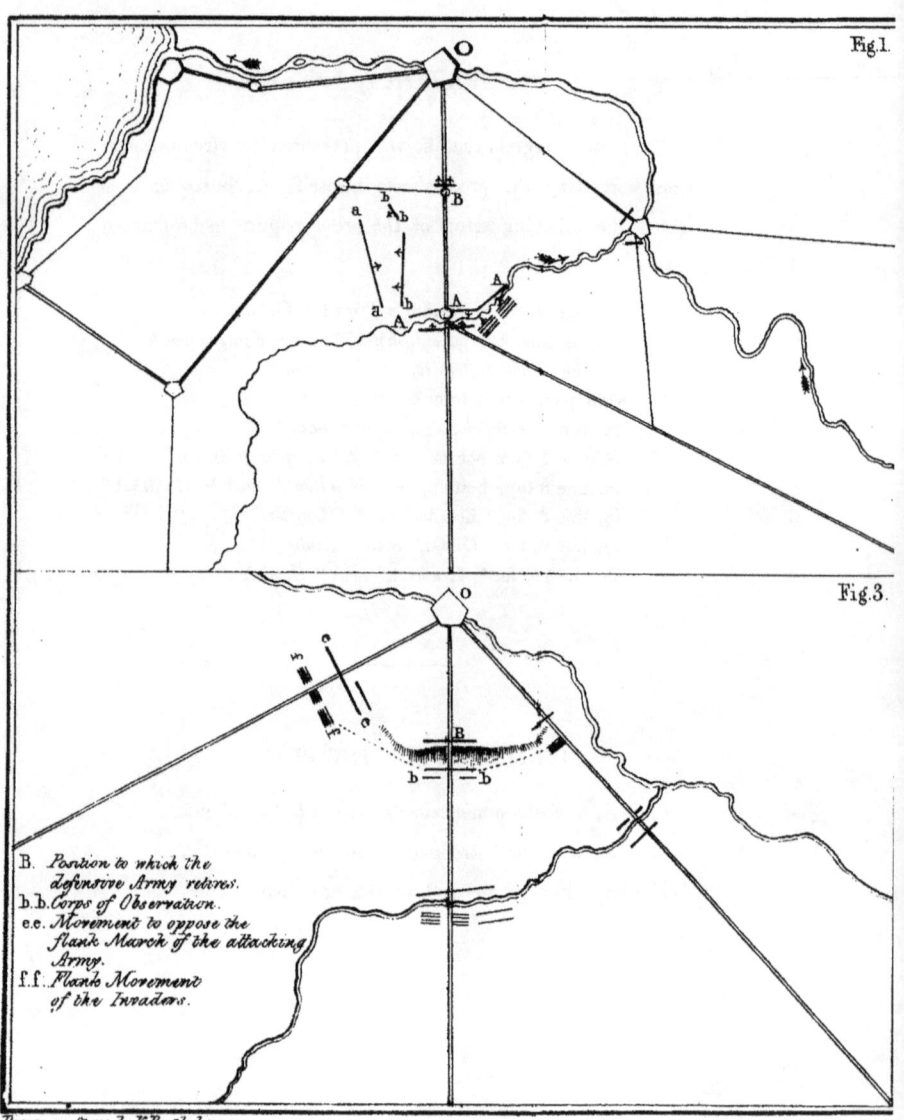

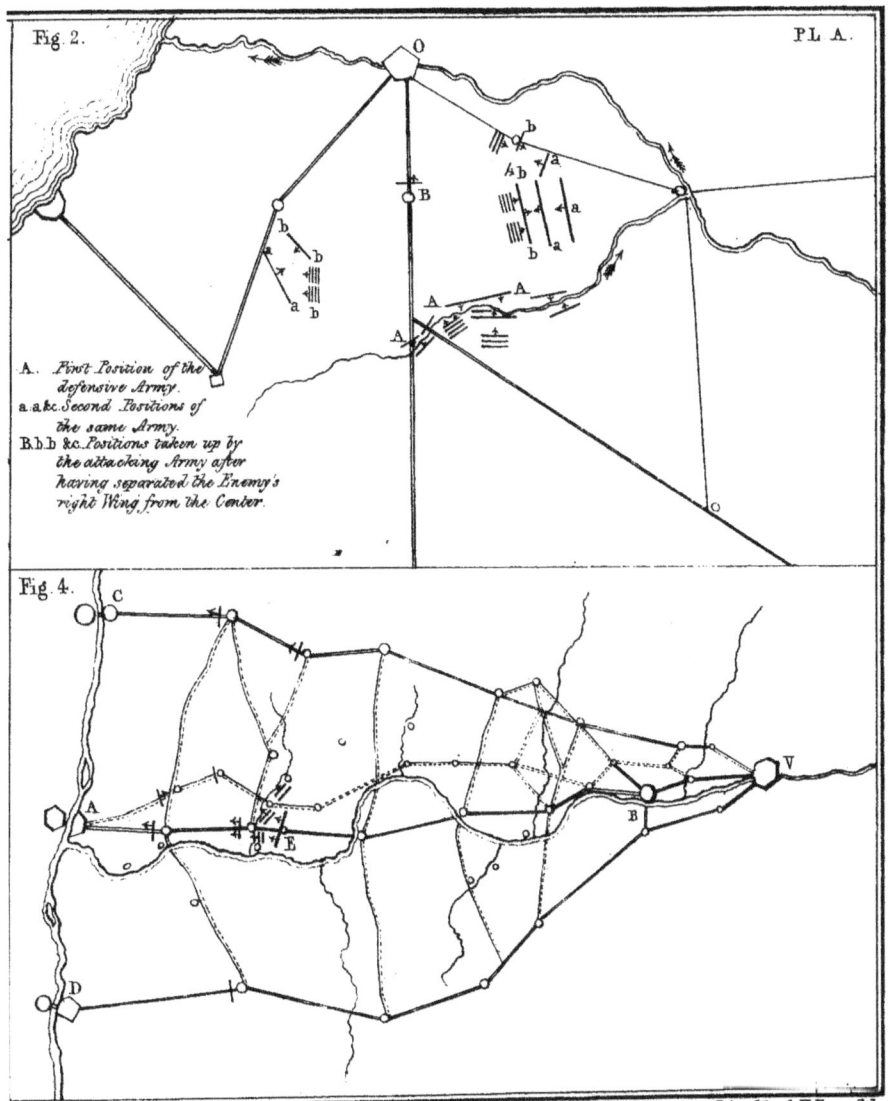

INTRODUCTION.

To imagine that a General could be formed by study alone, without the necessary experience, would be equally unreasonable as to expect that an officer should be capable of command, merely because he may have acted, for years, in the usual routine of duty, without accustoming himself to reflect on the true principles of his profession. In either case, it would probably be found, that he was placed totally out of his sphere, and that he would have to rely on his own judgment and decision at a time when the least hesitation may cause the most fatal consequences. But, when we come to examine with attention those instances in which a commander has suddenly raised himself to an equality with the most experienced generals, we shall uniformly find, that, independently of the advantages which he derived from the superior powers of his mind, by which he was at once enabled to perceive the mistakes of his adversary and impelled to profit by them, he has been guided by certain principles, in the observance of which a chief may reasonably look for success, whilst the disregard or contempt of them has ever led to defeat and discomfiture.

To endeavour to elucidate some of these principles, and to place them in a conspicuous point of view, is the desire of the Author of these Notes, in order that those who propose to follow the military career, may be led to the study of such writers as have treated on the subject in the most able and scientific manner; for it has been truly remarked, that, " in the same manner as the study of history leads statesmen to an acquaintance with people and governments, so does the attentive perusal of the history of campaigns of great captains become a fertile source of instruction for soldiers, under the twofold consideration of theory and practice, since their faults, being rectified by the true principles of strategy, tend to increase the experience of every attentive reader."

By accustoming himself to remark with attention every circumstance which may contribute to increase his knowledge, an officer will lay up in his mind a store of information which may serve him when he least expects it; whilst another, who suffers every incident to pass unheeded, will be as unfit to command at the end of ten years' service, as he was on the day he commenced his career. In short, some men will gain more real experience in a twelvemonth, than others in twenty times that period.

But, as theory cannot be better exemplified than by demonstrating how it has succeeded when acted upon in practice, we shall content ourselves with giving a few examples to introduce the subject, and then proceed to describe the manœuvres consequent on the Battle of Jena; than which a finer example does not exist upon record, to show the triumph of conduct over the total disregard of it, and to prove that, however we may contemn science and pretend to undervalue her instructions, she will always enable those who follow them to assert their superiority.

1. When we find a general acting on the defensive, we may naturally infer that his army is inferior, in moral or numerical

force, to that of his adversary. The object of the latter should therefore be, not only to force him to retire, in which case he might fall back on a position perhaps stronger than that from which he has just been driven, and all the blood spilt in the attack will be of no avail, whilst the same work remains to be done over again, but he should endeavour, at the same time, to separate the different corps composing his army, and to throw them off their line of retreat, and to get into such a position in their rear, or between the defensive army and the point which it has to cover, that the commander of it may be precluded from the hope of being able to regain his line of operation without fighting a pitched battle; in which case his former inferiority will tell more than ever to his disadvantage, whilst the road to the capital, or whatever point is to be attained, being left open, or but slightly guarded, detachments may be sent out to seize on the most important points, so that, even if the defensive army should, by good fortune, regain their line of operation, they will find themselves cramped and confined in their communications, whilst an active enemy in their front will not fail to seize the first opportunity to overwhelm them.

Suppose, for example, (figure 1, plate A,) an army be in position, A A, to cover a certain point it the rear, O ; it is clear, that if it can be forced by a judicious attack, as by turning a flank for instance, to retreat in the direction *a a*, whilst the enemy pushes on to B, and takes up his ground at *b b*, that the latter will be able to prevent the defensive army from communicating with the point O, unless by a more circuitous route, and that it is, consequently, cut off, and may be driven on an impassable frontier, such as the sea, or a chain of mountains of which the defiles are in possession of an enemy, &c., whilst at the same time the road is open to O.

2. If the commander of the attacking army have succeeded in forcing the centre of the position, (figure 2,) it follows that the situation of the defensive army will be worse than in the preceding example; the different corps being separated from each other, and they may consequently be beaten in detail.

These are, of course, extreme cases; but they have not, therefore, the less frequently occurred. For instance, at Baylen, in 1808, fourteen thousand French troops, under General Dupont, after a most determined effort to re-open their road to Madrid, were forced to lay down their arms to the Spaniards under General Reding. The same consequences were the result of the battle of Vimiera in the same year. A hundred other instances might be quoted.

3. Supposing (figure 3,) that the enemy, finding he will not be able to maintain his position, judiciously retires in proper time, so that he preserves his communications, and falls back on a point B., which he has caused to be strongly intrenched beforehand; the general commanding the attacking force may then leave a corps of observation at $b\,b$, sufficient to deceive the enemy and hold him in check, and make a flank movement to $f\,f$, which will oblige the enemy to leave his position at B, and move to e, e, in order to cover the point O; he may then be attacked with advantage, having been obliged to leave part of his forces in their former position, to prevent the advance of the corps of observation at $b\,b$.

4. In advancing on an enemy's territory, it is in general preferable to have but one grand line of operation, although it does not follow, from this principle, that the army is only to march by one road, nor that detachments may not be thrown out on either flank, to protect the march of the main body; on the contrary, both these arrangements are essentially requisite; but it is intended that only one *general direction* should be followed, and that the different columns should be within reach of assistance from each other, by cross communications. For example, (figure 4,) if the object be to gain possession of a certain point, V, as a capital city, for instance, it is better to move by one principal communication, from A to B, than to divide one's forces into three bodies, which should move respectively from three points, C, A,

D, at the distance of forty, fifty, sixty, or more, miles from each other, with a view to unite at a certain assigned point, B; because, although it might be imagined that the enemy would, in like manner, be obliged to oppose them by as many divisions of his own force, and that the retreat of one of these would ensure that of the rest of them, yet, a general who should take up a centrical position, as at E, would be enabled to impede the advance of each body, by a series of obstacles, such as intrenched positions, &c. in which a small force might hold a much larger one at bay for several days, and whilst, with the main body of his army, he should suddenly fall upon one of these columns, it would be almost impossible for the others to render it any assistance. This is easily conceived, because the enemy would have to make a flank movement upon the circumference of a circle, of which, the defender would be in the centre.

Besides, the want of concert, which would inevitably ensue from various causes, independently of the failure of communication by cross roads and the interception of messengers, would be alone sufficient to render abortive any enterprise grounded upon such principles. We have only, out of a hundred examples, to select that, so well known, of 1796, as described by the Archduke Charles of Austria.

Every success in war, must depend on the talent of the general who conducts the army; and, for this purpose, he must be perfectly unshackled by directions, from those, who, not being on the spot, cannot possibly judge of the exigencies of the case. He must hold his army, as it were, " in the hollow of his hand," and be ready to hurl it like a thunderbolt, at the point which his eagle-glance may descry to be most vulnerable. Implicit obedience in the subordinate commanders, and on the part of the troops the most perfect confidence in their leader, can alone enable the latter to execute any movement with that celerity and impetus which are requisite to insure its success. It is the duty of every man who presumes to call himsef *a soldier*, to make the best of the means he may possess, and he should be proud to supply, by his own activity and perseverance, any deficiency in the materials which may be put into his hand. Where the will is not wanting, the means will always be found.

These few examples may serve for the present, and we shall take occasion to remark, during the course of the narrative, upon such points as may serve to illustrate the subject, only observing, that it is not by a servile imitation, even of the chef-d'œuvre of a master, that we can hope to arrive at eminence; but by seizing the spirit and intention which have guided the greatest generals in their movements, a person may be enabled to apply them to the circumstances in which he may be called on to act.

Pl: B. OUTLINE of the Theatre of Operations, consequent on the Invasion of PRUSSIA, in 1806.

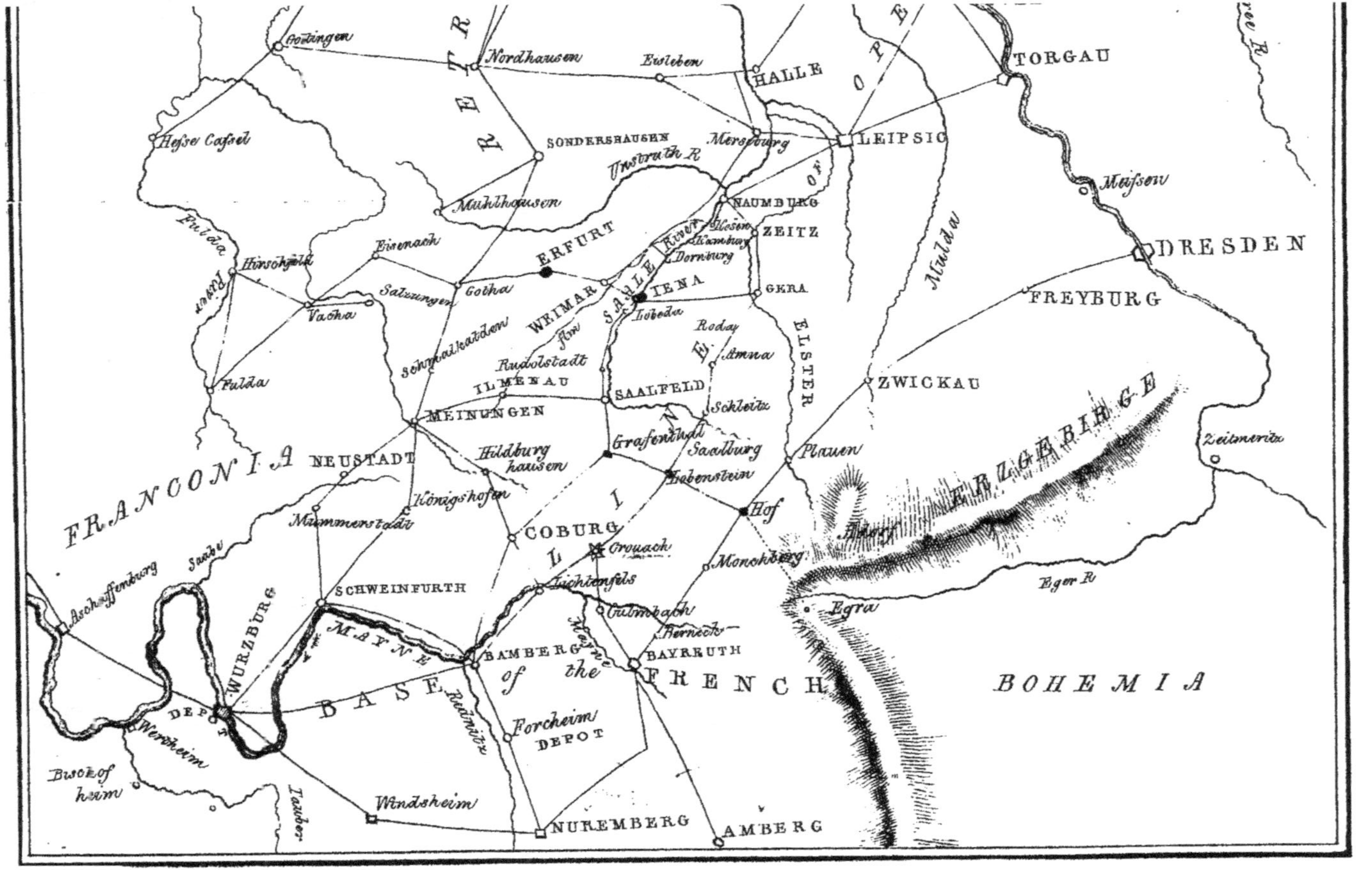

Drawn for the "Notes on the Battle of Jena" by I.H.H. on Stone by V. Bartholomew

Printed by C. Hullmandel

NOTES,

&c. &c.

NAPOLEON, victorious at Austerlitz, over the third coalition which had been formed for his destruction, saw himself, in a few months after the peace of Presburg, which followed that victory, in a condition to dictate laws to nearly the whole of continental Europe. The power of Austria was curtailed, and the emperor, despoiled of his finest provinces, was forced to renounce all claim to the sovereignty of the Germanic body; the French armies, cantoned from the Adriatic to the mouth of the Ems, kept down every attempt which might have been made by the German princes to throw off the yoke, which, however disguised, the modern Charlemagne had imposed on them; the Confederation of the Rhine divided that country against itself, and, by fomenting the jealousy which had always existed, on the part of the smaller states, towards Austria, it enabled their common enemy to turn their fatal disunion to the purposes of his own aggrandisement. Naples, deprived of her independence, was compelled to accept a king at the hands of her conqueror; and Holland hastened to beg the favour of being allowed to rank as a tributary kingdom, under the sceptre of a brother of the dictator, in exchange for the vain shadow of liberty which she had retained; whilst the armies of Russia, but just escaped from destruction on the banks of the Danube, were retracing the way which had led to the brink of ruin, utterly unconscious of the fate which was yet to overtake them in the fields of Eylau and Friedland.

In this state of affairs, and perceiving too late the snare into which she had been beguiled, when she accepted the sovereignty of Hanover in exchange for the territories of Anspach, Cleves and Neufchatel, Prussia found that she had been the victim of a system of policy by which she had expected to establish herself as the arbitress of the continent, and now discovered that her more wily adversary had only sought to involve her in a war with England, out of which he would never assist her but to subject her the more effectually to his own domination.

Thus deceived, humbled in her own estimation, and having an inheritance of glory to support, there remained but an appeal to arms, which could vindicate her honour and replace her in that station which ought ever to have been maintained, by a country whose princes were the heirs of the Great Frederick.

It would be quite foreign to the plan of the present work, to follow, through all its windings, the course of a diplomatic correspondence, during which each party must have seen that his adversary was seeking but to colour his own cause with the seeming hue of justice. It will be easily imagined, that the conqueror, who had but just deigned to declare in General Orders, " that the dynasty of Naples had ceased to reign," ere he sent his legions to sweep them off the throne, could not fail to perceive that he must seize the moment for action, ere his enemy could have determined on his own plan of proceeding.

His answer to the ultimatum of the Prussian minister was a proclamation to his soldiers, in which he reminded them " that they were about to march over those same Prussian battalions which, fourteen years before, had attempted to reach the capital of the Great Nation, but which had been obliged to desist from their rash undertaking, at the aspect of the irresistible grenadiers, whose wrath, again provoked, would prove more tremendous than the waves of the ocean when excited by the tempest!"

To doubt of success never entered into his contemplation, because we shall see that he did not neglect a single precaution which could tend to insure it. It is there that we perceive the true cause of all his successes. He led Fortune in chains, and she found herself compelled to proclaim his triumph; but the moment the fickle goddess found that the tie was loosened, and when *the neglect of his own principles* unbound Victory from his car, she flew to display her dazzling wings over the ranks of his enemies. Does the less glory result, on this account, to the brave soldiers who first dared to " beard the lion in his den," and to stem the torrent which had carried away in its course every obstacle which had hitherto been opposed to it? No.—He who would attribute such an inference to the writer, must have a soul which never delighted to contemplate the triumph of genius, which is equally worthy of admiration, whether it be found in a friend or a foe!

On the side of Prussia, the forces brought into the field amounted to 180,000 men, without reckoning the garrisons and militia which were dispersed in the several places out of the line of operations. The army consisted of three corps; that of the right wing contained 40,000 men, under General Rüchel, and was concentrated on the frontiers of Hesse-Cassel, in the neighbourhood of Mühlhausen.

The centre, or grand army, was commanded by the King in person, with the Duke of Brunswick as his lieutenant, and contained 70,000 men; it was formed behind the Elbe, in the district of Magdeburg, with its advanced guard on the Saale. Generals Möllendorf and Kalkreuth commanded under the Duke.

The left wing, or army of Silesia, united with the Saxon corps of 20,000, amounted to 55,000 men, under the command of Prince Hohenlohe. Prince Louis of Prussia commanded under him. The death of this brave and gallant soldier, the hope and the idol of the Prussian army, which happened at Saalfeld, as he was vainly endeavouring to retard the destruction which was advancing with rapid strides to overwhelm his unfortunate companions in arms, is one of the most affecting incidents of the whole war.

He fell gloriously on the field of battle; less

happy indeed than the Roman Curtius, since his devotion only served to render the ruin more irretrievable.

This army was cantoned in Saxony, with its advanced guard at Hof, its left supported on the mountains which form the frontiers of Bohemia. There was, besides, a detached corps of 15,000 men under General Blücher in Westphalia.

The whole army occupied a line of nearly forty leagues, from the neighbourhood of Mühlhausen to Hof. The Elbe was considered as the base of operation, and the places of Dresden, Torgau, Wittenberg, and Magdeburg, were made the principal depôts and points of support.

This distribution of the several corps was considered as well calculated either for the defensive, or for taking the lead in the offensive, as they might be concentrated in three or four marches at any point determined on, and might advance by either of the three principal communications, viz. on the left by Bayreuth, in the centre by Erfurth, and on the right by the valley of the Fulda. The ruin of the Prussian cause was to arise from the false movements which were afterwards made, from the want of unity and concert which existed in the ideas of the several generals as to the plan which was to be pursued, and from their acting on a totally wrong supposition of the situation of the French army. Napoleon, on the contrary, had decided in his own mind on what was proper to be done; the orders to the several generals were all at once, and in secret, transmitted to them; and we shall see that his enemy was literally surprised, before he had put himself in an attitude of defence. As a proof of the implicit obedience which he exacted, we will transcribe part of a letter from Berthier, his confidential *Chef-de-l'Etat-Major*, to General Marmont in Styria, about the time of signing the peace at Presburg.

He writes thus, " I have submitted your last letter to the Emperor, General; his majesty is offended at the observations you made, and charges me to say, that his orders are to be punctually executed; that all you say would be very well, if, in the first place, you had a division at Bruck, because you are neither acquainted with the projects of the Emperor nor the state of the question. *His majesty confides his designs to no one.*"

To understand the movements which are to be described, the reader must attentively trace them out on the map, as, without perceiving the objects of the marches which were made, it cannot be of the smallest consequence to know that a certain corps marched on a certain day, to such and such a position. But, to return to the Prussian army. Without having any plan definitively fixed and arranged to suit the circumstances, and which should have opposed the whole mass of the army to the bulk of the French troops, Prince Hohenlohe was ordered to march by the great road from Dresden, by Freyberg and Zwickau, into the country of Bayreuth. The object of this movement would seem to be, to pass the defiles of the forest of

Thüringia, and to place respectable forces at the sources of the Saale, the Eger and the Mayne, in the neighbourhood of Bayreuth, to meet the shock of the French army; whilst the centre, consisting of 70,000 men, should move by Gotha and Eisenach into the neighbourhood of Vacha and Fulda, and thus assume the offensive on both flanks of the forest, the intermediate defiles being guarded by detached corps. The army of General Rüchel, forming the right wing, was to cover the right of the other two, and act on the defensive.

This idea is said to have been in conformity with the opinion of Prince Hohenlohe, who wished to act independently, but who had justly imagined that the enemy would seek to penetrate, *en masse*, by the defiles of the Fichtel Gebirge (or Fir Mountain), against Saxony and the upper Elbe; because he would thereby have the most direct line of operation on Dresden and Berlin; because this line is the least protected by fortresses, and the possession of all the north of Germany depends on that of the towns on the upper Elbe. But it was, withal, very defective, inasmuch as the two principal bodies of troops would have been separated by a great interval, and no good can be expected to result from dividing one's forces when the enemy acts entirely in a body. But it was imagined that it would be sufficient to guard the passes on the left, and it was expected that the French would be surprised in their cantonments before they could be assembled under the Emperor. Vain supposition! which the experience of so many years might have dissipated, were it not for the extraordinary infatuation which seemed to possess all those who were in any way connected with this unfortunate campaign. Prince Hohenlohe's army was even weakened, by withdrawing ten battalions, twenty-five squadrons, and three batteries, to augment the centre.

The left wing was hardly in motion to execute the above-mentioned manœuvre, when counter-orders were received, in consequence of another plan which had been determined on at Headquarters, and which was to concentrate the left wing, by the 5th October, between Saalfeld and Jena. This plan appears to have been to the following effect. " The object is to cross the forest of Thüringia, to penetrate to the Mayne, and cut through the centre of the line which forms the base of the movements of the enemy, whilst the two wings shall be covered by two small corps of observation. That on the right will be the corps of General Blücher, and on the left that of General Tauenzien, in the neighbourhood of Bayreuth. Prince Hohenlohe will march in several columns in the space between Schleitz and Gera, so as to be, by the 5th October, between Saalfeld and Jena.

" The army will be, by the 10th October, between Ohrdruf and Saalfeld.

" General Rüchel, with the right wing, will be at Eisenach by the 7th October, and will push a strong detachment on Hünefeld, in order to give the enemy apprehensions for Fulda. General Blücher's corps will act with the right wing.

" The centre and left wing will pass the defiles of the forest on the 11th and 12th October.

" The centre will be at Neinungen on the 12th, and the left at Hildburghausen."

If the enemy previously sought to turn the left wing, the army was to have assembled in a camp on the heights near Hochdorf, in the neighbourhood of Blankenhayn, the right on the forest of Thüringia, the front covered by the defiles of the Saale; if the right wing was threatened, the army was to assemble near Mühlhausen, and to march on Göttingen. The corps of reserve under Prince Eugene of Wirtemberg, was to advance to Magdeburg.

By all this *tatonnement*, which we can scarcely find a name for in English, the very point by which the French army might penetrate with the fairest prospect of success was left open, the roads to Leipsic, Dresden and Naumburg were uncovered, and, in fact, the Prussian army left its communications with its principal depôts exposed, and turned its flank, and almost its rear, to the advance of the enemy.

This change of direction caused great confusion in the left wing, and was with difficulty followed. The columns crossed each other's path, and the quarters and supplies were interfering with each other, which should always be avoided at the opening of a campaign, as it destroys both the discipline and confidence of the troops, and prepares them for defeat.

The Head-quarters of Prince Hohenlohe were at Jena on the 2d October, and those of the King, at Erfurth, on the 4th. No certain information had as yet been received of the movements of the enemy. It was understood that a corps was assembling at Neustadt on the Saale, in Franconia, and that Marshal Augereau's corps, the imperial guard, and the reserves, were marching on Aschaffenburg, where the Emperor was also expected. All these reports, with others equally unconclusive, induced the Prussian Generalissimo to conclude, that Napoleon intended to concentrate his army behind the Saale in Franconia, and to await the attack of his enemies.

However at variance with the well-known character of the French General such a determination might have appeared, this opinion was pertinaciously maintained until intelligence was received on the 7th, that a considerable corps was assembling at Bamberg, and that the French were advancing on Hof in such force, that General Tauenzien, if attacked, would be forced to fall back on Kahla or Jena, and the road to Leipsic be thus left open. Even this information did not suffice to induce a change of measures, and orders were issued to be ready to cross the defiles on the 9th. On the 8th a dispatch from the Duke of Weimar confirmed the intelligence of the French having quitted the neighbourhood of the Saale in Franconia; a reconnoissance had been made as far as Neustadt on that river, and had found the position completely abandoned, with the exception of a small garrison in Königshofen. The same report also gave information, that the whole French army was directing its march on Bamberg, and that the intention was evidently to turn the left of the Prussians in Saxony. The project of crossing the forest of Thüringia was now of necessity abandoned, although it was too late to repair the error, for the enemy was at that moment on the point of attacking the advanced guard at Saalburg, which was the next day to be routed at Schleitz. However, under the idea of retarding the movement of the French, the Duke of Weimar was ordered to move out and support an attack of light cavalry, which was to be made on the 10th on the columns in march behind the Mayne. Alas! that day was to be remembered as one of the most ill fated to the Prussian arms. In the meantime the army was ordered to assemble in the following positions, viz. the centre in a camp near Hochdorf, as before-mentioned; the left wing was to fall back to the left bank of the Saale, the movement not having been yet completed.

General Rüchel, with the right wing, was to be at Erfurth, and the Duke of Weimar was afterwards recalled. The reserve under Prince Eugene of Wirtemberg was directed to move on Halle. The King's head-quarters were fixed at Blankenhain.

Having now, to the best of our information, described the uncertain movements and counter-marches of the Prussians previously to Napoleon's attack on their advanced guards, we must sketch the positions of the French armies in Germany, and show how they were concentrated for the advance on Jena, which it has been thought best to defer until the present moment, that the reader might have a clear idea of the situation in which Napoleon caught his enemy, as it were *in flagrante delicto*, and scattered his columns, like chaff before the wind, in every direction but that which they would have wished to follow in their retreat.

By the conditions of the Peace of Presburg, the French troops were to be withdrawn from the Austrian territories by the 2d March following (1806); but, until all the articles of the treaty should be fulfilled, the French Emperor determined to keep possession of the fortress of Braunau on the river Inn, which would also serve to keep Austria in check, in the event of any fresh war breaking out in Germany; an event which Napoleon probably anticipated from the opposition which Prussia could not fail to offer to the changes which he was about to introduce in the ancient constitutions of the German empire.

Marshal Soult's corps (the 4th) was accordingly distributed in the three places of Braunau, Passau, and Landshut, whilst the rest of the troops, which had been employed in the preceding campaign, were cantoned in Bavaria and Swabia, so that they might, in a few marches, be moved up into line on the banks of the Inn. Berthier, as Lieutenant of the Emperor, and *Chef de l'Etat Major,* or Quarter-Master-General of the Grand Army, established his head-quarters at Munich. This threatening attitude was preserved by Napoleon in order to facilitate his political views with regard to the Confederation of the Rhine; and when he began to perceive a war with Prussia inevitable, under various pretences, such as alleviating the burthen imposed on the states in the neighbourhood of the Danube, and facilitating the subsistence of the troops, the several corps of the army were gradually drawn more together in the districts of Nuremberg and Wurtsburg, so as to be concentrated in a moment at any point which might be required to march on Leipsic and Dresden.

On the 3d October, the day on which Napoleon arrived at Wurzburg, and the Prussian head-quarters were at Erfurth, the French army was in the following positions; the generals commanding the several corps having received orders to that effect some time previously, so as to be enabled to arrive on the appointed day at the posts from which they were simultaneously to concur in the general movement, which was to be executed under the direction of the General in Chief.

Marshal Soult, with the 4th corps, of 41,000

men, after having provided for the defence of the line of the Inn, for the particulars of which the reader is referred to the order in the Appendix as worthy of being studied, had been directed to move on Amberg, and to take up a position between that place and Bayreuth.

The 6th corps, of 33,000 men, under Marshal Ney, was at Nuremberg.

The 1st, consisting of 23,000 men, under Bernadotte, Prince of Ponte Corvo, was at Lichtenfels, with its advanced posts in front of Kronach, and in the debouches leading from Coburg.

Marshal Davoust, with the 3d corps, of 33,000 men, was at Bamberg.

At Schweinfurth was posted the 5th corps, of 22,000 men, with advanced posts in the debouches round Königshofen and Neustadt (on the Saale, in Franconia). As this corps was, two days afterwards, placed under the command of Marshal Lannes, we shall call it by that name, although it was previously under Lefebvre, who was then posted to the infantry of the guard.

At Wurzburg, the head-quarters, there were the 7th corps, of 19,000 men, under Marshal Augereau, and the imperial guard, of 9,000 men, under Marshal Bessières. The reserve of cavalry (20,000), commanded by Muràt, Grand Duke of Berg, was quartered on the line behind the Mayne, from Wurzburg to Kronach, ready to move in any direction in which it might be required. By observing this distribution on the map, we shall find that the army, consisting of 209,000 men, was formed in three grand masses; that on the right, containing Soult's and Ney's corps, amounted to 74,000 men, in front of Nuremberg, and was ready to debouche on Hof: the centre, composed of Bernadotte's and Davoust's corps, amounting to 56,000 men, was to march on Kronach and Lobenstein: and the left, at Schweinfurth and Wurzburg, amounted to 50,000, and was to move by Coburg on Gräfenthal. The reserve of cavalry and the imperial guard complete the number. The contingents of the Princes of the Confederation amounted to 26,000 men, and were in second line.

As the left column was, in a manner, the foremost in the advance, we shall begin by describing the route which it followed, and by which it prepared the way for those on its right, to converge on it as a pivot, and to form the line on the flank of the enemy.

Marshal Lannes, already distinguished as the *intrepid* hero of so many victories, led this column with the 5th corps. After having passed, on the 8th and 9th October, by Coburg and Gräfenthal, the defiles of the mountains which form the frontiers of Saxony, he arrived in the morning of the 10th on the heights of Saalfeld, and prepared to attack the enemy under Prince Louis of Prussia, who was determined to defend the pass, with eleven battalions, eighteen squadrons, and three batteries, being convinced that Napoleon's object was what has been already stated, and wishing to give time to unite the army between the Saale and the Elster to oppose the execution of it.

The resistance was obstinate, but hopeless. The Prussians were overpowered, Prince Louis was killed in the *melée* as he was endeavouring to save the retreat of his troops, who fled in disorder, leaving 1,200 killed, 1,800 prisoners, 4 standards, and 33 pieces of cannon, with their equipage.

In the centre, Marshal Bernadotte, with the 1st corps, and Muràt, with a brigade of light cavalry of his reserve, having passed the defiles leading to Lobenstein, marched on the 8th to attack the enemy at Saalburg, a strong post, which was occupied by two battalions and two squadrons, detached from the corps of General Tauenzien, who was himself in position at Schleitz, two leagues in the rear of it, with ten battalions and eight squadrons. The detachment, perceiving that the French cavalry was preparing to pass the Saale below the village, and apprehending their retreat would be cut off, evacuated the post, which was surrounded by a wall flanked with towers, and retreated on their main body. General Tauenzien advanced a short distance and remained, during the day, in position along the edge of the wood of Oschitz, but fearing for *his* retreat, he retired again during the night on Schleitz. On the 9th he was attacked, routed, and driven back on Mittel Pöluitz, leaving 500 killed and wounded, besides 300 prisoners, and 2 guns. The French did not lose above 100 men. The next day (10th) Bernadotte fixed his head-quarters at Auma; Muràt with his cavalry marched on Gera, where he arrived on the 11th, having picked up, on his way, a convoy of 500 carriages, including ammunition waggons, bridge equipage, &c. &c.

Davoust followed at half a day's march in the rear, and took up successively at Saalburg, Schleitz and Auma, the positions which the 1st corps had quitted. On the 11th he was ordered to oblique to the left towards Mittel Pöluitz, in order to converge on Naumburg. Napoleon himself had directed the march of this column, and was present at the first action. His headquarters were on the 9th at Ebersdorf, on the 10th at Schleitz, and on the 11th at Auma.

On the right, Soult occupied on the 9th the town and environs of Hof, which Tauenzien had been obliged to evacuate in order to avoid being cut off at Schleitz by the centre column of the French. On the 10th the Marshal proceeded to Plauen, when, finding that there was no corps of the enemy in that direction towards Dresden, he marched on Weida, and occupied Gera on the 12th. Ney, following at half a day's distance in the rear, marched on the 10th and 11th by Tanna and Schleitz, and arrived on the 12th at Auma.

Thus the whole French army was already nearly united between the Saale and the Elster, in the very position which the Prussians and Saxons should have taken up to cover their communications on the Elbe. The most fatal consequences could not but be apprehended from the defeat of the two advanced guards at Schleitz and Saalfeld, in which, as will always be the case in similar circumstances, the troops of the two allied nations (who, by the way, have ever hated each other most cordially) mutually laid the blame on each other, when in fact it arose chiefly from the ill-direction which was given to their efforts.

As long as any appeal remains from the decision of the general-in-chief, so long will uncertainty, error and defeat, follow the movements of an army. The troops will find themselves beaten in spite of all their efforts, and even if one corps is victorious, it will have to retire because another is unsuccessful. The difference of opinion among the different generals, which was allowed to influence the operations of this campaign, enabled the enemy to fall upon the army before it was in an attitude of defence, and the want of information as to his movements is equally extraordinary, when we reflect, that the peasantry and citizens were the countrymen of the defenders, and therefore ought naturally to have been the more anxious to afford them any information which they might be able to give. It is also a proof of the incontestable superiority which the French staff officers possessed over their rivals.

Whilst the two advanced guards were thus beaten as related, Prince Hohenlohe was in march to fall back on the position behind the Saale, where the King was waiting to unite with him and General Rüchel. On the 10th, in the afternoon, he learnt the news of the affair at Schleitz the day before, and, shortly afterwards, that of the ill success at Saalfeld, and of the death of the Prince. He hastened to take up a position at Kahla and Roda, to cover the retreat which was to be continued next day. A false alarm, occasioned by the crowd of fugitives thronging in, threw the whole camp into the utmost confusion and disorder, and by retarding the arrangements for the intended movement, it contributed not a little to its further ill success.

Napoleon was continuing his movement, with the centre, on the road to Leipsic, and hastened to concentrate his forces in that direction, so as to cut off the enemy from the Elbe, and at the same time he kept himself ready to attack him in front, if he held out between the Saale and the Elster.

On arriving at Auma on the 11th, and finding that the Prussians were still in the direction of Erfurth, he sent orders to the chiefs of the several corps to direct their troops as follows, viz.

To the Grand Duke of Berg, (Muràt,) who was at Gera with his cavalry, to set off immediately for Zeitz, to push out scouts on Leipsic and Naumburg, and to march rapidly on the latter point if he learnt that the enemy was still in the direction of Erfurth.

To Marshal Soult, to occupy Gera.

To Marshal Ney, to move up to Auma.

To Marshal Davoust, to move on Naumburg, to send his light cavalry first, and to send out scouts to make prisoners and gain intelligence. His corps (the 3d) was reinforced by a division of dragoons under General Salin.

To Bernadotte, to follow Muràt by Zeitz to Naumburg.

To Lannes, to march instantly on Jena, to send scouts towards Weimar, and to gain all possible intelligence of the enemy since the affair at Saalfeld.

To Augereau, to march on Kahla, to correspond with Lannes, and to send scouts on Blankenburg and Magdala to gain intelligence of the enemy.

These orders were punctually executed during the 12th and 13th October, and the Emperor received at Gera, during the night of the 12th and morning of the 13th, the reports which he had required. The most important was that of Marshal Lannes. Moving on Jena by the road from Rüdolstadt, on the left bank of the Saale, he had met in the afternoon of the 12th, near Winzerle, a strong advanced guard. He had attacked it with his light troops, had driven it back, and had halted for the night behind the village. The next morning at daybreak, (13th,) notwithstanding the fog and the defiles of the road, he had pursued the enemy, who retired on their main body. Arrived at Jena, he had turned the town by the valley called the Mühlthal, and crowning the heights with his tirailleurs, he had discovered the whole Prussian army disposed in three lines.

Napoleon being now certain that the whole of the enemy's forces were beyond the Saale, had no doubt that the King's army, united with Prince Hohenlohe's, was in presence of Marshal Lannes, and, in order to attack them and profit by the bold reconnoisance of the general, he had scarcely any changes to make in his preceding dispositions.

Marshal Soult was, at that moment, with the Emperor, who pointed out to him in few words his plan of attack, and the part which the 4th corps was to take in it. He at the same time ordered him to move it up as quickly as possible from Gera to Jena.

Ney was at the same time ordered to bring up his corps (the 6th,) from Auma to Roda.

Davoust and Bernadotte, who would be by

that time at Naumburg, and who were to act together, were ordered to manœuvre on the left of the enemy.

Marshals Lefebvre and Bessières, with the Imperial Guard, arrived that evening at Jena.

Muràt was at Zeitz, to which place he had fallen back, having taken a second convoy of 300 artillery waggons.

Napoleon himself, after having expedited these orders by successive officers, went to Jena, passed through the town, and arrived about four o'clock in the afternoon on the Landgrafenberg, where Lannes had posted the advanced guard.

Having brought the reader thus far, let us pause for a moment, and, ere we describe the two memorable battles which were fought at Jena and at Auerstädt, on the following day, let us consider the respective situations of the hostile armies, and the chances of success which each might reckon upon.

Napoleon had encompassed his adversary in such a manner, that, let him manœuvre as he might, he had no escape but in victory; whilst on his own part, he was at liberty either to attack him in his present position, or to pursue his march on Leipsic or Halle, and the Elbe, whilst his retreat was secure on Forcheim, by the same road which he had used in his advance.

The Prussian army, on the contrary, whose only chance of safety consisted in remaining united, and the principal part of which, that morning's dawn had seen in position between the Saale and the Ilm, to the number of 122 battalions, 172 squadrons, and 300 pieces of artillery, was now divided, and pursuing a flank march in presence of the enemy, and taking up its quarters for the night in perfect ignorance of the impending storm.

Prince Hohenlohe had remained in position on the heights to cover the rear, and considered Lannes's attack on the Landgrafenberg in the light of any thing but the forerunner to the general action which was to ensue.

Imagining that the French army was in full

march on Leipsic, the king had that morning moved by his left towards Auerstädt, intending to pass the Unstruth, and then, being covered by the Saale, either to fall back on the Elbe and unite with the reserve, or else to march on the rear of the enemy, whilst the Duke of Wirtemburg should have opposed the passage of that river. He was not aware of the strength of the corps at Naumburg, nor of the impossibility which existed of executing the contemplated movement across the Elbe.

General Rüchel was in position behind Weimar; and after having suffered the enemy to penetrate between the Saale and the Elster, the whole army could not have been perhaps, better placed than it was when its advanced guard was first attacked at Winzerle. The valley of the Saale in that neighbourhood is extremely deep, and covered with wood, and totally impassable to an army, except at the points of Lobeda, Jena, Dornburg, Camburg, and Kœsen, so that by taking a position, as the Prussians and Saxons had done, at a certain distance in the rear of it, they might have fallen upon each column of an approaching army, and utterly prevented any deployment. We have now to return to Napoleon, who bivouacked in the centre of his guard, and disposed every thing in such a manner, that on the following day, as the sun mounted the heavens, and dissipated the mists of the morning, he should see his enemies fade away like the darkness which now interposed between them and destruction.

The Emperor had perceived, at the first glance, the importance of the point on which he stood, and he disposed Suchet's division, forming the right and centre of the 5th corps, with its right on the ravine called the Rauh-thal, two regiments being in second and third line behind the centre, whilst General Gazan's division, on the left, lined the head of the ravine opposite Kospoda, and 4,000 of the guard, under Marshal Lefebvre, formed a square behind the centre, in the midst of which Napoleon had his tent. The remainder of the evening, and the whole of the night, were employed in getting the artillery up the road called the *Steiger*, for which purpose it had to be widened and rendered practicable by the greatest exertions. During the night the Emperor, riding with Soult and Suchet to observe more nearly the position of the enemy, was fired on by an advanced picquet, which he had passed by without perceiving it, but luckily escaped unhurt. Until the next morning, it appears that Prince Hohenlohe, whose head-quarters were at Kapellendorf, had no apprehension of a serious attack, or, at all events, he imagined that he had only Lannes's and Augereau's corps in front of him, in which case he could not but desire an engagement, having the advantage on his side. The Duke of Weimar was at Ilmenau, the King at Auerstädt, and Prince Eugene of Wirtemberg between Magdeburg and Halle.

The French army bivouacked in the following positions, ready to start up at the first crowing of the cock, to pursue the attack; Davoust, with his corps, (3d,) at Naumburg, his advance occupying the defile of Kœsen; Bernadotte, with his corps, also behind Naumburg; Soult's corps in front of Jena, ready to debouche by the Rauh-thal on the right of the 5th corps on the Landgrafenberg, as before-mentioned; Augereau's corps on the left in the Mühlthal, (valley of Mills,) and on the Galgenberg (Gibbet Hill); Ney, with 3,000 of his corps, round Jena; whilst Muràt, with 70 squadrons of his reserve, was on the road between Camburg and Dornburg.

The action was commenced in the morning by Marshal Lannes, who formed his corps partly in line and partly in column, and led it against the village of Closwitz, which was occupied by the enemy. The fog was at first so thick that it was impossible to distinguish any thing, but towards 9 o'clock, the atmosphere clearing up, discovered the corps of General Tauenzien along the wood, and occupying the village. The position was carried, and the 5th corps formed in two lines in front of Kospoda, between Closwitz and Lutzerode, 22 pieces of cannon having been taken in the affair.

Soult was at the same time advancing up the Rauh-thal and the Zwetschen-thal, out of which defiles and woods he drove all the enemy's tirailleurs, and directed his left on Closwitz. The enemy, driven out of this position, rallied on the heights in front of Rödchen, on the right, and the Saxon division, under General Holtzendorf, charged the right of General St. Hilaire's division, (of Soult's corps,) which was advancing to attack them. A charge of the Prussian cavalry was received at a few yards' distance by a volley from the 10th light infantry, and the cavalry being charged in turn by Soult's *chasseurs à cheval*, was routed and driven out of the field. The general was then forced to retreat, being cut off from the centre, and retired to the heights of Stobsa, leaving six guns with the French. He was kept from uniting with the main body all the day, and afterwards retreated by Appolda across the Ilm, where he lost a battalion of light infantry and ten more guns.

The success of these first attacks gave the Emperor room to deploy his masses, and to bring up the left wing and reserves (6th corps and guard).

The greater part of the 6th corps, (Ney's,) which during the night had bivouacked near Roda, was detained in the narrow roads leading to the Landgrafenberg and the village of Kospoda, but the marshal himself hastened forward with his grenadiers and light troops, and his brigade of light cavalry. He arrived on the field between 10 and 11 o'clock, and, passing through the centre of Lannes's corps, he moved against the village of Vierzehn-Heiligen (the 14 Saints).

Augereau's corps (7th) had moved at daybreak from its bivouacs on the Galgenberg and in the Nühlthal, and was defiling by the road from Jena to Weimar. To take up its ground on the Floh-berg, and in order to allow the artillery and cavalry the benefit of the road, the infantry of the brigade, which headed the column, climbed up the sides of the hill and formed at top, whilst the second brigade followed the road up the defile. As soon as this division (General Desjardin's) was united, it formed in two lines beyond Kospoda; the other division of Augereau's corps (under General Heudelet) continued to move along the bottom of the valley, by the road to Weimar, to attack the Saxons, who were in position above the *Schnecke*, behind the ravine called the *Schwabhauser-Grund*.

These were the first dispositions of Napoleon to drive in the advanced corps of the enemy, who disputed every foot of ground, but who was, notwithstanding, forced to retire at every point.

The French troops were, by mid-day, in line, as nearly as the form of the ground either permitted or rendered necessary, and were then moved up to the attack of the enemy, who had taken post on the heights behind 14 Heiligen, the right wing, composed of the principal part of the Saxon corps, being beyond the valley of Isserstädt.

The attack of the French on the villages of 14 Heiligen and Isserstädt, and of Augereau at the Schnecke, were all successful, as they could not but be, with the advantages of number which they possessed. The centre being forced, the Saxons were cut off, and, being the last to retreat, they suffered dreadfully. The next day 300 Saxon officers and 6,000 men, prisoners, were restored to their country, the forced alliance of which with Prussia was dissolved, and they remained faithful allies of the French until the very last.

The reinforcement under General Rüchel came up too late to be of any service : the rout was complete; and the several corps retreated in the greatest disorder across the Ilm, principally at Denstädt. Muràt's heavy cavalry had not been able to arrive in time to participate in the action, and was immediately sent in pursuit of the flying enemy. The victorious army bivouacked on the field of battle; Soult with his corps in the environs of Schwabsdorf; Ney, who had been joined by his two divisions, occupied the town of Weimar; Lannes remained at the fork of the roads between Jena and Naumburg, near Umpferstädt; one of his brigades, however, pursued the enemy as far as Weimar, and bivouacked at Ober Weimar; Augereau's corps took up its ground on the left of the town, and Napoleon returned to Jena.

Prince Hohenlohe had rallied beyond Weimar twenty squadrons of cavalry to cover the retreat of his troops. When he saw them flying in all directions, and that he could not oppose any effectual resistance to the pursuit, he commenced his march for Büttelstädt, having been led to believe, from a false report, that the King had gained a complete victory at Auerstädt. He was, however, quickly undeceived, for he received a letter from the King, informing him of the total ill success of that part of the army, of the Duke of Brunswick and Marshal Möllendorf being mortally wounded, and that he was retreating on Weimar and Erfurth. Now this line was already intercepted at Weimar, and the French cavalry was also in march for Büttelstädt. The Prince, in this dilemma, took an intermediate course, and retired with his cavalry on Schloss Wippach, four leagues to the north of Weimar, and the same distance from Erfurth and Büttelstädt.

Napoleon had yet to learn the better half of his good fortune; that an army of nearly 70,000 men, headed by the King of Prussia in person, had been beaten and forced to retreat by one of his lieutenants with his *corps d'armée* of 27,000 men.

We have endeavoured, thus far, to describe in a concise manner the movements which were executed by the two armies, and we have discarded all circumstantial details and considerations which might prevent the reader from perceiving at a glance the positions of the several corps of each commander; but the description of the battle of Auerstädt, which is to be found in Count Dumas's History, is so much to the purpose, that it cannot be curtailed or altered without detriment; we shall therefore transcribe it almost literally, and afterwards make such remarks as may suggest themselves upon an attentive consideration of the narrative.

It has been already stated that the King of Prussia, with the Duke of Brunswick, had marched in the morning of the 13th to their left, intending to pass the Unstruth. The column was composed of five divisions; the 3d, under General Schmettau, being at the head, was followed by the 2d, under General Wartensleben, and by the 1st, under the orders of the Prince of Orange. The reserve, consisting of the divisions of Generals Arnim and Kanheim, closed the march. General Rüchel was to follow at the distance of a day's march in the rear, and General Blücher, who was acting with Rüchel, had been ordered to join the King and to command the advanced guard, as the Duke of Weimar, having been detached across the forest of Thüringia, was too far off to arrive in time for that command.

General Schmettau having attained the heights of Appolda, and hearing a cannonade in the direction of Jena, halted his column, but the officer, whom he sent to reconnoitre, reported that it was some unimportant affair. It was, however, the attack of Marshal Lannes on the Landgrafenberg, as already described, when he followed the advanced guard he had met at Winzerle the evening before. The general, therefore, continued his march, and his division took up its ground, at 6 o'clock in the evening, on the heights between Auerstädt and Gernstädt, supporting its left on the wood of Lisdorf. The battalion of grenadiers of Schacke was placed on the left in front of Eckartsberg, and the advanced posts were reinforced by the queen's regiment and a battery of horse artillery. The divisions of Wartensleven and Orange, and the reserve, bivouacked in two lines, with the right in front of Eberstadt, and the left in rear of Ranstadt, forming a salient angle at the point where the high road crossed them. These four divisions arrived successively at their bivouacs from 6 o'clock until midnight. As they had not been able to provide themselves with rations at Weimar, they had no other food than the little they could collect in the adjacent villages, whilst the French were plentifully supplied from the magazines they had taken at Naumburg; a circumstance which military men well know how to appreciate. The King, with the Duke of Brunswick, established his head-quarters at Auerstädt.

During the evening a party of cavalry detached from the advanced guard, met a French patrol of six men on the road beyond Auerstädt, and another of thirty horse chasseurs near Hassenhausen, a league from Kösen. The Prussians took two prisoners, and learnt that the bridge at Kosen had not been destroyed, and that Naumburg was then occupied by a corps under Marshal Davoust. This general, who with his escort had advanced to the top of the hill above the defile to reconnoitre the ground and the position of the enemy, should he discover any, rallied the chasseurs, and drove back the Prussian detachment. The two prisoners were conducted to Auerstädt and interrogated by the Duke of Brunswick, who thought, notwithstanding, that the information was not to be relied on, and that the communications could only be intercepted by small detachments. In consequence, the order was given to continue the march the next day, in order to pass the Unstruth and take up a position behind it, fronting the Saale. The 3d division was to advance to Kösen, to cover the flank of the column which was to pass behind it, and cross over at Lancha.

This division, which had first arrived in position, and was only two leagues from the defile of Kösen, might easily have seized this important point, which ought to have been done, even as a preventive measure, against any aggression during the flank march. Never was the necessity of a forced march more clearly pointed out; nevertheless, the advanced posts were not pushed beyond Gernstädt, whilst Marshal Davoust returned to Naumburg, and sent two battalions to occupy the village of Kösen. The next morning he sent for his generals of divisions to give them his orders, in conformity with those he had received from the Emperor at 3 o'clock. They were dated at 10 o'clock the evening before, from the bivouac on the heights of Jena. Napoleon mentioned that it was his intention, the next morning, to attack the Prussian army, united, as he thought, in front of Weimar, and he ordered the marshal to march on the rear of that army. He left him the choice of the road, provided he took a part in the action. The tenor of these orders proved, that the Emperor intended to turn the left of the enemy; he could not foresee that the greater part of their forces had moved off, and were then in front of the corps which he destined to make this diversion. He added, " if Marshal Bernadotte be with you, you may march together, but the Emperor is in hopes he will be in the position pointed out at Dornburg."

This general had arrived at Naumburg with his corps, (1st,) which was bivouacked behind the town, whilst that of Davoust was ready to pass the defile of Kösen. The two marshals might therefore have marched together on Appolda, by the left bank of the Saale; nevertheless, the 1st corps must have waited till the 3d had passed, and time might consequently be saved by starting at once for Camburg or Dornburg, and then crossing the river and marching on Appolda, the two corps would have found themselves united.

Davoust waited on the Prince of Ponte Corvo, (Bernadotte,) and communicated the orders he had received, at the same time proposing to him to pass after the 3d corps, and then to take the command of the two united, so that it was not from any jealousy or misunderstanding that he was left to contend alone with the King of Prussia's army. But Bernadotte thought himself obliged to march the three divisions, which formed his corps, to Dornburg, because that position had been first indicated by the Emperor, and he accordingly put his troops in motion. We shall see, that he was not able to arrive until the action at Jena was finished, and the Prussians were retreating from Auerstädt.

The Saale in that part is not fordable, and the left bank is very steep, and covered with tufts of wood. The high road from Naumburg to Weimar and Erfurth, is by the stone bridge at Kösen, which is the only pass, whence the road winds up a long and steep acclivity to the level of Hassen-hausen. On account of the distance at which his 1st division was placed in the rear, the marshal ordered the movement to be commenced by the left. The 3d division, under the orders of General Gudiu, passed the bridge at 6 o'clock in the morning, whilst Colonel Cassagno with the two battalions which had occupied the post during the night, rapidly traversed the defile, and, preceded by a squadron of chasseurs, debouched on the plateau. The 2d and 1st divisions, put in motion at 4 o'clock in the morning, directed their march on the same point.

On the side of the Prussians, the King, who had ridden to the bivouac of the foremost division (Schmettau's), sent for General Blucher, and, until the troops which were to form the advanced-guard should be assembled, he ordered him to take five-and-twenty squadrons, with a battery of horse artillery, and to drive back any cavalry of the French, which should have advanced beyond the defile. Blücher put his troop in motion at six o'clock, and Schmettau's division followed.

A thick wet fog prevented any thing from being seen beyond the distance of a pistol shot. Marshal Davoust having passed the defile with his staff, at the head of the column, sent forward one of his aides-de-camp, Colonel Burke, with a detachment of chasseurs, and ordered him to engage a skirmish for the purpose of making some prisoners in order to gain intelligence of the position and force of the enemy. The colonel, having passed the village of Hassenhausen, without meeting either vidette or advanced post, suddenly found himself within a few yards of Blücher's advanced guard, with which was the King in person, and which, perceiving the French detachment through the fog, called a halt. The French fired their pistols at the enemy, and sustained the charge of two squadrons which advanced upon them. Having taken some prisoners, among whom was a major, and thus fulfilled their mission, they retreated as fast as possible, and rallied under the protection of the 25th regiment, which was advancing in column on the right of the road, whilst the 85th moved on the left of it.

General Gauthier, commanding this brigade, formed the squares to receive the Prussian cavalry, and placed his artillery across the road, in the centre. Blücher, with the remainder of his cavalry, his light artillery, and a battalion of grenadiers, advanced past Hassen-hausen, after the squadrons which had pursued the French detachment; but being severely galled by the fire of case-shot and musquetry, which was poured upon them, the squadrons and grenadiers were broken and thrown into disorder, and the captain commanding the battery and most of the gunners being killed or wounded, the drivers scampered off with the limbers, and the French took possession of the guns. The 25th regiment then advancing, sustained a second charge of cavalry, and took, in the same manner, a second battery of artillery, which had been brought up against them.

This vigorous resistance, and subsequent attack, surprised the Prussians: the Duke of Brunswick was of opinion, that the army should be formed up, and the march suspended, until the fog cleared off and discovered the force of the enemy. Marshal Möllendorf, on the contrary, thought that they could have but inconsiderable forces in front of them, and that it was advisable to move on at once and drive back into the defile whatever troops might oppose them. The King being also of the latter opinion, the duke sent orders to the two divisions behind (those of Wartensleben and Orange), to quicken their pace, and to move on the left of the village of Hassen-hausen, and reconnoitre the force of the enemy. But the fog precluded the possibility of discovering beyond a very short distance. Schmettau's division was by this time in line facing the village, and Blucher's cavalry formed on its left.

Davoust, perceiving that this cavalry extended beyond his right and threatened to turn it, moved up general Petit's brigade, as soon as it arrived on the right of the village, and the 85th on the left. The light infantry occupied the village, and, together with the fire of the artillery, galled the Prussian line severely, and they placed ten more pieces of cannon on their right.

The action being thus warmly commenced, Blücher sought to turn the right of the enemy, by Spielberg and Punscherau, and the fog clearing up a little, he perceived he was on the flank, and in rear of the French infantry. He immediately charged, and if successful, this charge would have decided the affair; but the French, having in time formed squares in echellon, received the cavalry with such a close discharge, that the latter renewed their attacks again and again without success. The combat was warm and bloody. The marshal and his generals, passing from one square to the other, in the intervals of the charges, animated their troops to a steady resistance, and not a battalion was broken. At length, after having lost a great proportion of their numbers, all this cavalry was forced to fly, which it did in great disorder, pursued off the field by the squadrons of the French, which had arrived on the plateau, and formed by Punscherau. Blücher himself, having a horse killed under him at the moment, with difficulty escaped upon that of a soldier, and was carried away in the crowd.

During this time, upwards of an hour and a half, the King of Prussia was pressing, by repeated orders, the march of the 2d and 1st divisions, which were delayed in passing the defile of Auerstädt. This sovereign, whose personal valour deserved better success, was on the left of the line, at the head of Wartensleben's regiment, which suffered most from the fire of the French, who now had the decided advantage on their right, where they drove the Prussians out of Spielberg; but on their left they were so outnumbered, that it is difficult to conceive how the Prussians failed to annihilate them. Their tirailleurs were most excellent, and appear to have had a sort of instinctive perception of their profession. They had a large share in the success of more than one general action during the ascendancy of Napoleon's star, when by their well-directed and destructive fire, and their boldness in advancing on the flanks of an enemy, they thinned his ranks and determined the fortune of the day.

The efforts of the Prussians were now directed against the left of the French line, which had hitherto been the weakest. Much time was, nevertheless, lost, in forming up the divisions as they arrived, and in dressing their lines, and several regiments were so thinned by the fire from the village, that they were dislocated and gave way before they could reach it to attack the French who occupied it, and whose infantry and artillery were greatly protected by the houses and enclosures from the fire of the assailants.

At this critical period of the action the Duke of Brunswick received his mortal wound, and, at the same moment, General Schmettau received a second one, which also obliged him to quit the field, and shortly terminated his life. General Wartensleben had his horse killed, and not being able for some time to find another, the line was deprived at once of nearly all its chief commanders. The remaining divisions of the French now arrived, it being near 10 o'clock, and reinforced the left of their line. Prince William of Prussia tried the same manœuvre against this part of the French line which Blucher had attempted against their right, but his attacks were received in the same manner by the several regiments in squares, and the destruction of this superb cavalry was quite beyond precedent. The prince himself was wounded, and the cavalry being routed off the field, it was of little further use in the attack during the whole day.

The French now turned the tables on the enemy, and General Friant moved up between Spielberg and Zechwar, whilst his tirailleurs penetrated to Poppel and Tauchwitz, and thus completely turned the left of the Prussian line, and forced it to retreat. General Billy was mortally wounded in this advance.

The Prussians had now suffered great loss, and the retrograde movement of the left exposed the flank of the centre, which was also obliged to fall back, and was in turn followed by the right.

The object of the French marshal being to cut off the enemy from the woods and the heights, and to turn their left so as to throw them on the Saale, it was essential that he should consolidate his own left in such a manner that they might not be able to force it, and thus open the way to Kösen. For this purpose he must occupy the heights of Rehausen and Sonnendorf, which are on the extremity of the plateau, and he might then proceed to attack the Prussians in the position to which they had fallen back. If he succeeded in this, the enemy, whose left wing was already beaten, would be forced to abandon their position in front of Auerstädt, and would be intercepted by the main body of the French army which was in their rear; which event actually followed.

The Prussian generals were well aware of this circumstance, and therefore reinforced their right by fresh troops drawn from the reserves. A column composed of the Weimar chasseurs, a battalion of fusileers, and two regiments of guards, advanced by the village of Sonnendorf near Rehausen, whilst some companies of tirailleurs filed up the little valley. The King personally superintended this attack. This prince, since the Duke of Brunswick had been carried off the field, had been in the thickest of the action, and his horse had already been shot under him. As the French had no cavalry on their left, he endeavoured, by a last effort, to force through the infantry, which was gaining ground on the heights, and he would afterwards have turned the flank of General Gudin's division, which was driving into the valley of Rehausen the wrecks of Wartensleben's and Schmettau's divisions.

Marshal Davoust perceived the object of this

manœuvre of the enemy, and he ordered General Morand himself to hasten with the artillery of his division to the heights on the extreme left by Sonnendorf, towards which the 30th regiment, and the 1st battalion of the 17th had already been directed. The general, supported by these two regiments, charged and drove back the Prussian columns, which had been overwhelmed by the fire of the artillery, and forced them to retrace their way across the valley. He then continued to advance, and gained the extremity of the plateau, where he placed his guns in a commanding position, which flanked and cut up the whole of the enemy's line, and determined the retreat of the divisions which had been beaten.

The attacks on the villages of Spielberg and Poppel had been attended with great loss to both parties, and the Prussians had a thousand men surrounded in the latter village and taken prisoners, with several pieces of cannon. The wings being thus victorious, Davoust attacked the village of Tauchwitz in the centre, whilst the three divisions of the Prussians, which had been beaten, were retreating by the diverging roads of Eckartsberg, Reisdorf, and Auerstädt, with the loss of half their numbers, having left the greater part of their artillery on the heights of Hassen-hausen.

General Kalkreuth advanced with the two divisions of reserve, which, since the commencement of the action, had remained in line between Auerstädt and Gernstädt. He formed his line behind Tauchwitz and Rehausen, with the rivulet in his front. His right rested on the valley of the Emsen-Mühle, and his left extended beyond the heights opposite Poppel, and was flanked by a brigade of grenadiers, hastily collected, under the command of Prince Augustus. All the cavalry, rallied under the orders of Marshal Blucher, was in the second line, a few squadrons being placed on the wings of the infantry, and the artillery in front.

This line was still respectable, and the undaunted veteran proposed to renew the action with his cavalry, but, after having remained some time in this attitude, the Prussian general found he should be obliged to retire to his former position behind Gernstädt, his right wing being overwhelmed by the enfilading fire of General Morand's artillery, whilst his left was equally incommoded by the advancing batteries of General Friant on the opposite hill beyond Poppel. At the same time the French troops, having already occupied Lisdorf, were advancing on Eckartsberg.

Marshal Davoust, having seen his left firmly established on the Sonnenberg, had gallopped to the right, which was now, by its converging movement, deciding the victory. He directed General Gudin's division in the centre to conform to the general movement, and, debouching by Tauchwitz and Poppel, he directed it himself on the left of the heights of Eckartsberg.

Towards 4 o'clock, after nine hours continual fighting, the French had nearly turned the left division of the reserve, which then marched by its left in front of Eckartsberg, protected by a large battery of artillery. Whilst General

Grandeau, at the head of the 11th regiment, advanced on the plateau by the right, General Gudin's division attacked in front, and 400 men, under the direction of General Petit, rushed on the guns in the teeth of their fire. The Prussians abandoned with precipitation this last position, and left twenty-two pieces of artillery in the hands of the assailants, who pursued them beyond the wood and castle of Eckartsberg. The French left wing passed the valley and charged the right of the reserve, which had suffered from the fire of the guns on the Sonnenberg. The cavalry retired by Auerstädt, and, after having passed the defile, it formed afresh in face of the village, which was occupied by a rear guard, but a battery of howitzers quickly set it on fire, and forced the Prussians to abandon it.

The regiments of the guards made their retreat in good order along the heights on the left bank of the Ilm by Wickerstädt, vigorously pursued by the battalions of General Morand's left, which had passed the valley. The rest of the Prussian divisions continued their retreat in the directions already mentioned, and the action ceased about 5 o'clock.

The French having lost a third of their numbers, and having no cavalry on the left and in the centre, whilst that of the enemy covered the plain and protected the retreat of their infantry, Marshal Davoust was unable to follow up his success in a satisfactory manner. Nevertheless General Viallannes continued to harass the left flank of the retiring enemy, and the marshal ordered him to endeavour, as much as possible, to throw them towards the Saale and in the direction of Appolda, so as to cut them off from their proper line of retreat.

During this pursuit General Viallannes took many prisoners and several pieces of cannon, and drove the scattered parties of the enemy as far as Büttelstädt, where he bivouacked his squadrons. Marshal Davoust united his divisions between Eckartsberg and Auerstädt, and passed the night on the field in the midst of his troops.

The King of Prussia, who was quite unaware of what had taken place at Jena, had resolved to fall back on the corps of Prince Hohenlohe. He passed through Auerstädt at the head of his cavalry, intending to arrive rapidly at Weimar, and make dispositions for a general action on the following day. The army was following the direction of the high road, great confusion necessarily attending such a retreat, when, on approaching Malstädt, they perceived a line of watchfires crowning the heights of Appolda, and extending across their line of retreat. They were those of Bernadotte's corps, which had set off from Naumburg at 3 o'clock in the morning in order to pass the Saale at Dornburg, and to act upon the left of the enemy, which was imagined to be at Appolda. But the difficulties of the road had been such, that the marshal was only able to arrive with one division on the heights in the evening, when both actions were terminated.

This unexpected rencounter forced the Prussian army to change its line of retreat. During the darkness of the night, terror and confusion achieved the dispersion of the columns which had escaped the swords of the enemy. Small parties, platoons and regiments, wandered at random through cross roads, every moment crossing and hindering each other in their uncertain march. The cavalry, not being able to leave the beaten track, was kept more together, but the regiments were nevertheless intercepted in their retreat, and not a horseman crossed the Oder.

The King, at the defile of Wickerstädt, had taken with him his own regiment and a battalion of grenadiers, and he now quitted the high road to Weimar, and took a direction more to the right. He did not arrive until the night was far advanced at Sommerda. During this arduous march, in which he was obliged to make several changes of direction, he learnt the news of the affair at Jena, and could judge by the reports which reached him at Sommerda, of the total dispersion of the three corps of his army. The next day he gave the command of the army to General Kalkreuth, and retired to Sondershausen.

The loss of the Prussians at the battle of Auerstädt was reckoned at 10,000 men, but the confusion of their retreat, and the events which ensued, did not allow of any exact return being made. Official reports own the loss of 324 officers, killed or wounded; among whom were the Duke of Brunswick, Marshal Möllendorf and two of the king's brothers, besides General Schmettau. The latter general, with the Duke and Marshal Möllendorf, died of their wounds; the marshal was eighty-one years of age. Marshal Davoust's corps lost 270 officers, and 7,000 under-officers and privates: General Gudin's division alone lost 134 officers and 3,500 soldiers, being half the total number who were put *hors de combat*.

Thus was achieved on the 14th October, 1806, the dispersion of that army which, directed by the genius of a Frederic, had astonished the world no less by its incomparable fortitude in reverses, than by its brilliant valour and its exact discipline in the hour of battle. On the very fields of their former glory the Prussian soldiers saw their hard-earned laurels destined to add new splendour to the brow of their conquerors, and although they afterwards nobly retrieved their fame in many a bloody field, they were for a time compelled to submit to that fate to which by turns all are subject.

Sixty standards, three hundred pieces of artillery, and immense magazines, were the trophies of five days of hostilities, and whilst Napoleon saw his enemy in full retreat before him, he might repose with security in the conviction, that not a battalion was to escape his victorious grasp. In fact, after a series of arduous and destructive marches, and frequent and sanguinary conflicts, Prince Hohenlohe, finding himself cut off by superior forces from the last point at which he had hoped to effect the passage of the Oder, was obliged to capitulate at Prenzlow on the 28th October, or only fourteen days after the battle. Sixteen thousand infantry, and six regiments of cavalry, the remains of what he had led out of action, laid down their arms to Marshal Lannes and Muràt, delivering up forty-five colours, and sixty-four pieces of artillery. On the same day another column, of four regiments of infantry and six of cavalry, was also surrounded in the same direction. The veteran Blucher, being in a similar manner cut off from Stettin, retraced his steps, continually pursued by his indefatigable adversaries, until, arrested by the frontier of the Danish territory, he must either have surrendered, or perished sword in hand. In this difficult alternative he determined to seize upon the town of Lubeck, hoping to defend it against all assault. The ancient fortifications had been partly razed, but solid ramparts, and deep impassable ditches, still held out a delusive hope of security. Ere four-and-twenty hours had elapsed, the French, surmounting every obstacle, and rushing through the cross fire of all the artillery that could be brought to bear on the gateways, entered the town sword in hand.

On that day, the 6th of November, this devoted city underwent all the horrors of a storm. Thirty thousand infuriated soldiers spread themselves over the place, and revenged, on the unoffending inhabitants, the obstinate resistance of their unwelcome guests. The Prussian general, being driven from this last hold, retreated with the few troops, chiefly cavalry, which he could collect, and was obliged to surrender the next day at Ratkau to the French marshals, Muràt, Bernadotte and Soult.

All the smaller columns were in a similar manner intercepted, whilst the corps of reserve, under the Prince of Wirtemberg, lost 7,500 men in defending the passage of the Saale at Halle.

The fortresses, which, honourably defended, might have impeded the progress of the victorious enemy, were pusillanimously delivered up, with hundreds of cannon, and whole arsenals full of warlike stores.

Napoleon entered Berlin as a conqueror ten days after the battle; the 3d corps, as a recompense for their bravery at Auerstädt, led the way, and encamped beyond the city.

The battles of Pultusk, Eylau, Friedland, &c., were the consequences of the Russian army advancing to renew the campaign, and the Peace of Tilsit (7th July, 1807) concluded the war of the fourth coalition.

In searching for the causes of this remarkable catastrophe, we are not less struck by the singular situation of the two armies, than by the good fortune which contributed, in such an extraordinary manner, to the decisive success of the French commander. The Prussians, ignorant of the exact situation of the invading force, nevertheless knew that Napoleon was on the direct line to Leipsic, Wittenberg and Berlin, so many points which it was their chief object to cover, and on which they depended for their supplies of ammunition and provisions. Napoleon, finding that the united Prussian and Saxon army was still behind the Saale, perceived at a glance, that, if he left it in that position, he would be in a very unsafe predicament, and be liable to have his communications interrupted. It was, moreover, his first object to gain a victory, and then to follow it up, so as to leave the enemy neither time nor opportunity to rally. Of success he did not doubt, for he knew his troops, and the power he possessed over them, and he had the advantage of the offensive as well as in point of number. The unlooked-for and ill-timed separation of the three corps of the allied army, delivered them up bound into his hand. At Marengo he had been attacked in his position before Desaix's corps was able to arrive to his support: at Jena he attacked the enemy, depending on Davoust and Bernadotte to co-operate on their flank; and although the latter was prevented from taking a part in the action, and several thousand heavy cavalry of Muràt's reserve only came up in the moment of pursuit, yet the intrepid resistance of the third corps at Hassenhausen, kept the main body of the enemy from pursuing their march, and forced them back on the point at which, instead of support, they found a gulph open to receive them.

But whilst we endeavour to derive a useful lesson from the mistakes and disasters of others, let us beware how we rashly condemn a proceeding, of which we can only judge by the unfortunate result, and at the same time that we admire the glorious issue of such scientific combinations, let us reflect that it is easy to judge after fortune has decided the victory, and that operations in war are influenced by many causes which never appear on the surface.

APPENDIX.

Order to Marshal Soult for the defence of the Inn and the occupation of Braunau.

Munich, 24th Sept. 1806.

MARSHAL SOULT will leave the whole of the 3d regiment of the line in Braunau, under the orders of General of Division Merle. Adjutant Commandant Lomet, a colonel and six officers of engineers under him, a colonel and four companies of French artillery, a squad of workmen, a company of sappers, four or five officers of artillery attached to the garrison, and two commissaries, will also be left there, and a regiment of cavalry.

The citadel of Passau will be armed and provisioned; it will be guarded by a Bavarian battalion.

The fortress of Kuffstein will be armed and provisioned; it will also be guarded by a Bavarian battalion.

The body of the Bavarian army, about 15,000 strong, will take a position between the Inn and the Iser; it will have advanced posts entrenched in the chateau of

Burghausen; it will keep patroles along the Bavarian frontier, so that the garrison of Braunau may not be insulted with impunity by the Austrians.

Marshal Soult will repair in person to Braunau, as well as the general officers of artillery and engineers, and a commissary, appointed by the Intendant General of the army, in order to inspect the state of the ammunition and provisions of all kinds which may be in the place. Every thing which may be wanted will be sent there, and the most positive orders given that the daily consumption of the garrison of Braunau may be furnished from Munich, so that the magazines in the place may be reserved for the moment of a blockade, if it should so happen. The duty in the garrison will be regulated in the strictest manner.

A Bavarian battalion, which is intended to remain in garrison with the French troops, will be encamped on the left bank of the Inn, at the head of the bridge of Braunau: a tête-de-pont will be constructed there, traced in such a manner as to be protected by the fire of the place, and which should be preserved, even if the place were shut up, and the enemy on the left bank of the Inn.

The marshal will fix upon a cipher, with General Merle, which will be communicated to the Major General of the Grand Army (Berthier).

There are to be in Braunau provisions for eight months.

General Merle will choose, as his second in command, a general of brigade, who may enjoy his confidence, and who might supply his place in case of accident.

Thus General Merle will have under his orders
3,000 of the 3d regiment of the line.
400 artillery.
100 sappers.
800 Bavarian battalion in the tête-de-pont.
100 Bavarian artillery, forming a company.
4,400 men, besides the regiment of cavalry.

With such a fine garrison, having provisions for eight months, and abundantly supplied with artillery; having among the engineers none but chosen officers, who are known as desirous of distinguishing themselves; and, above all, having two or three months to spare, during which every thing may be done to improve the place, the most brilliant resistance may be made; and in no case is the garrison to be given up, without having sustained several assaults in the body of the place.

A quantity of wood will be immediately brought from the Tyrol: *with wood, tools and hands, a fortress might be made where none existed before.* At Braunau there is the advantage of water and advanced works; and lines of counter attack may be made to prolong the defence until succours might arrive.

For the rest, nothing indicates that Austria entertains hostile views, and affairs must be managed accordingly.

Nobody is to enter the town, not even travellers; the governor is never to go beyond a cannon shot from the place, he is never to dine out of the town, and, when he goes out, the second in command is to be on the ramparts.

The pay of the garrison is to be secured for three months, and the money required for this purpose is to be lodged with the paymaster. The work to be executed by the soldiers is not to be paid for, and cannot be; it is dishonouring the soldier, who is to perform a duty of this kind from honour alone. The best understanding will be kept up with the Bavarians.

Posts will be planted at a cannon shot from the place, bearing an inscription, " Territory of Braunau." No body of foreign troops is to enter it with arms. The governor will communicate with prudence with the French minister at Vienna, and is to take care that in case his letters should be intercepted, they may not compromise anything. He is to send every day to

Munich, and to the major general, a report of what may come to his knowledge.

Above all, Marshal Soult will recommend to him, as well as to all the officers of the garrison, that they are to live on good terms with the Austrians, though on their guard.

Dispositions relative to the Place of Wittenberg.

Wittenberg, 23d Oct. 1806.

GENERAL CHASSELOUP will point out, in the course of this day, a spot on which ten ovens may be built. This spot must be near the magazines of flour, which are to contain a million of rations. The intendant general will cause the ovens to be instantly constructed, and will name a storekeeper to regulate the affairs of the magazines and of the carriages bringing the flour.

General Chasseloup will also point out a magazine to contain six hundred thousand bushels of oats.

He will appoint a place for the arsenal, at a short distance from a place where the waggons, and other incumbrances of the park, may be put. The general of artillery will immediately establish his forges, stow his ammunition, and park his carriages.

General Chasseloup will appoint a place for the powder magazine, and for a laboratory. These spots will be in the interior of the town; all the powder will be immediately taken thither.

The general of artillery will cause to be brought from Dresden thirty or forty battering pieces, with their carriages, platforms, &c., to arm the place.

The artillery will immediately prepare fascines, gabions, &c., to make the batteries on the ramparts.

The space between the town and the river will be closed as soon as possible with palisades, independently of the ditches, parapets and other works which the engineers may judge necessary. The general of engineers will take measures to procure a quantity of fir palisades, which will be easily done by detaining all the floats on the Elbe, and fetching down all which are above the town and on the river. Barriers will be constructed as soon as possible in front of the gates. Instead of drawbridges, which would require too much time to construct, bridges on trestles will be made, which may be thrown down in case of emergency. He will procure at least five or six thousand workmen for these purposes, and to introduce the water into the ditches, to repair the parapets, and to clear the scarps.

The surveyors will take plans of the ground to the distance of 1200 toises, on both sides of the river.

The square in the town will be kept quite clear of carriages, for the movement of the troops.

General Chasseloup will point out a building capable of holding twelve or fifteen hundred prisoners, so that they may always have a place to hold them as they arrive. The town and bridge will be lighted, and particularly the square. There will be two hospitals appointed, one for five hundred wounded, and the other for the same number of sick. Six depôts will be also appointed, one for each corps of the army, each to hold two hundred men.

The major general (Berthier) will make it understood at Paris, Mayence, Wurtzburg, Cronach and Erfurth, that everything which may be sent to the army, for whatever corps it may be, is to be sent to Wittenberg, where the scattered parties coming from hospitals and detachments will unite, at the depôt of their own corps, in this town. There they will be inspected by the governor, armed if requisite, provided with ammunition, and sent to their several corps according to the orders of the major general, and by routes which will be provided them. Orders will be given to the six marshals commanding the corps of the army, and to the Duke of Berg (Muràt) commanding the reserve, to direct on

Wittenberg all men fatigued and who require rest. Each corps will name a staff officer, who will remain with the depôt of his corps, and superintend their payment and discipline. All the soldiers slightly wounded will be directed on Wittenberg, where they will remain the number of days requisite for their perfect recovery.

His Majesty, *therefore, expects, that from to-morrow there will be no stragglers,* and that all the lame and knocked-up men will be sent to Wittenberg for recovery.

A printing press will be at Wittenberg and French printers, where everything required for the service will be printed.

Order of Battle at Jena.

Jena, 14th Oct. 1806.

MARSHAL AUGEREAU will command the left; he will place his first division in column on the road to Weimar, as far as the elevation by which General Gazau has moved his artillery on to the plateau; he will keep the necessary forces on the plateau on his left even with the head of his column; he will have tirailleurs along the whole of the enemy's line, in the different openings of the mountains. When General Gazan shall have advanced, he will debouch on the plateau with his whole corps, and will then march according to circumstances, to take the left of the army.

Marshal Lannes will, at day-break, have all his artillery in the intervals, in the order in which he has passed the night.

The artillery of the guard will be placed on the height; and the guard, drawn up in five lines, will be behind the plateau: the first line, composed of chasseurs, crowning it.

The village, which is on our right, will be crowned with the whole of General Suchet's artillery, immediately attacked and carried.

The Emperor will give the signal; it is to be expected at the break of day.

Marshal Ney will be ready at the peep of day to march up on the right of Marshal Lannes the moment the village shall be taken, and room thereby given to deploy.

Marshal Soult will debouch by the roads which have been reconnoitred on the right; he will unite, and keep always united, to form the right of the army.

The order of battle in general will be in two lines, without reckoning the light infantry; each line distant 100 toises at most.

The light cavalry of each corps of the army will be at the disposal of each general, to be used according to circumstances.

The heavy cavalry, when it arrives, will be placed on the level, and will be in reserve behind the guard, in order to be sent where circumstances may require.

The object to-day is to deploy in the plain. The dispositions will afterwards be made according to the force and manœuvres of the enemy, in order to drive him from the positions he may occupy.

Summary of the Strength of the different Corps of the French Army on the 1st October, 1806.

IMPERIAL GUARD.

Marshals, LEFEBVRE,
        BESSIERES.

Staff	345	
Grenadiers and light troops . . .	3,703	
Ditto cavalry	2,150	9,307
Dragoons, dismounted	2,397	
Artillery	712	

1st Corps, under BERNADOTTE.

Generals of Division, RIVAUD,
     DROUET,
     TILLY.

Staff	138	
1st division	6,049	
2d division	6,211	
Light cavalry	2,567	23,654
1st division, heavy cavalry	3,571	
4th do. dragoons	3,807	
Park of artillery	1,311	

The 2d Corps was in Italy.

The 3d Corps, under DAVOUST.

Generals of Division, MORAND,
     FRIAND,
     GUDIN,
     VIALLANNES.

1st division	11,100	
2d do.	8,971	
3d do.	9,570	33,198
Cavalry	2,643	
Artillery	914	

4th Corps, Marshal Soult.

Generals of Division, Saint Hilaire,
     Legrand,
     Leval,
     Margaron.

Staff	44
1st division	8,834
2d do.	11,683
3d do.	11,210
Light cavalry	2,710
2d division, heavy cavalry	2,281
3d do. dragoons	3,552
Artillery	714

Total: 41,108

5th Corps, Marshal Lannes.

Generals of Division, Gazan,
     Suchet,
     Treilhard.

Staff	19
1st division	wanting
2d do.	11,990
3d do.	7,695
Light cavalry	2,736
Artillery	344

Total: 22,784

(85)

6th Corps, MARSHAL NEY.

Generals of Division, DUPONT,
MARCHAND,
MALHER,
COLBERT.

Staff	49	
1st division	8,141	
2d do.	9,220	
3d do.	9,646	33,572
Light cavalry	1,347	
2d division, dragoons	3,833	
Artillery	1,326	

7th Corps, MARSHAL AUGEREAU.

Generals of Division, DESJARDINS,
HENDELET,
VICTOR,
AUGEREAU,
DUROSNEL.

Staff	13	
1st division	7,030	
2d do.	7,252	19,361
Light cavalry	1,519	
1st division, dragoons	3,169	
Artillery	378	

8th Corps, under MARSHAL MORTIER,
at Mayence.

Reserve of cavalry under Muràt, Grand Duke of Berg; with generals Lasalle, Milhaud, Nansouty, d'Hautpoul, Klein, Grouchy, Beaumont, Sahue.

1st and 2d divisions of heavy cavalry }
1st, 2d, 3d, and 4th divisions of dragoons } 20,693
Reserve and park of artillery, Gen. Songis . 5,683

THE END.

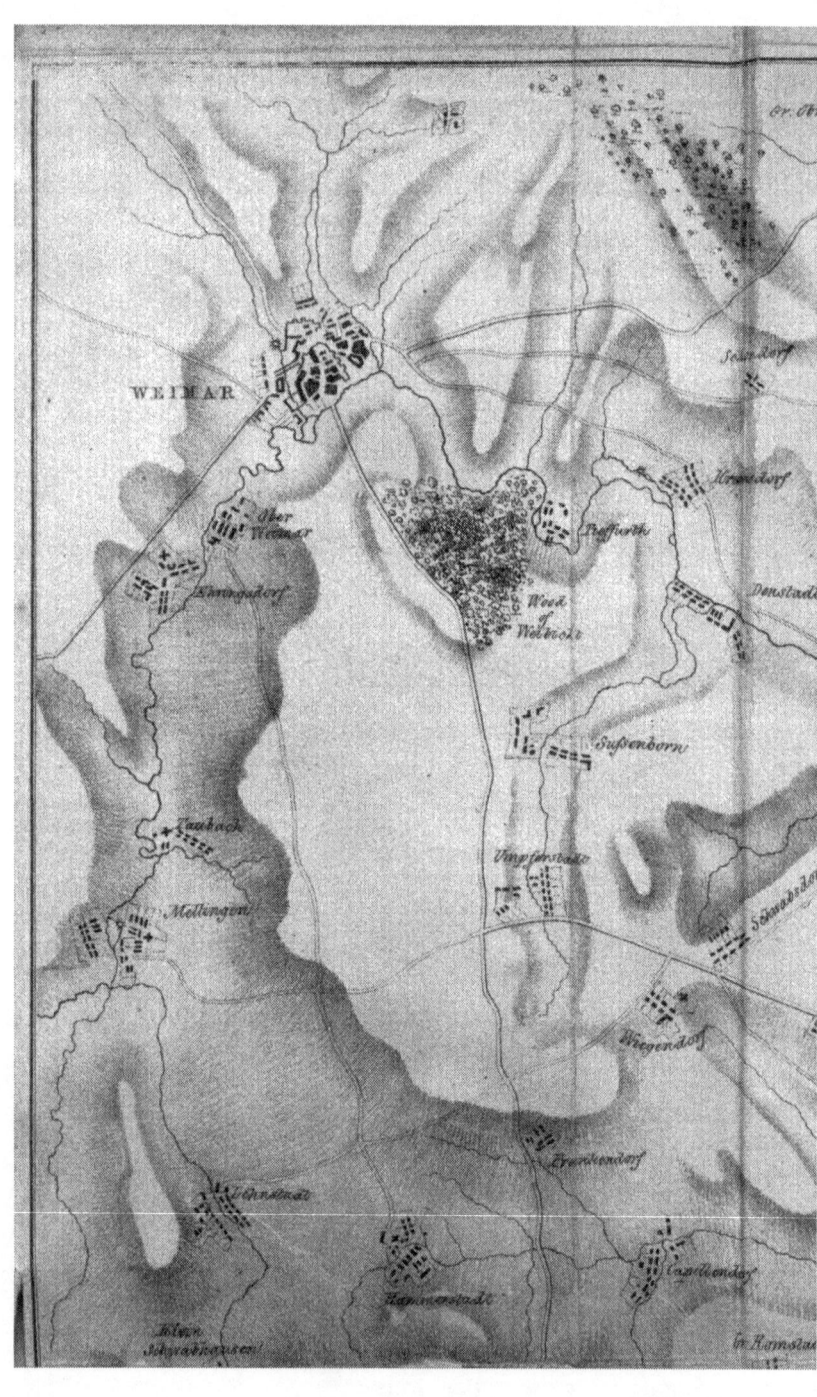

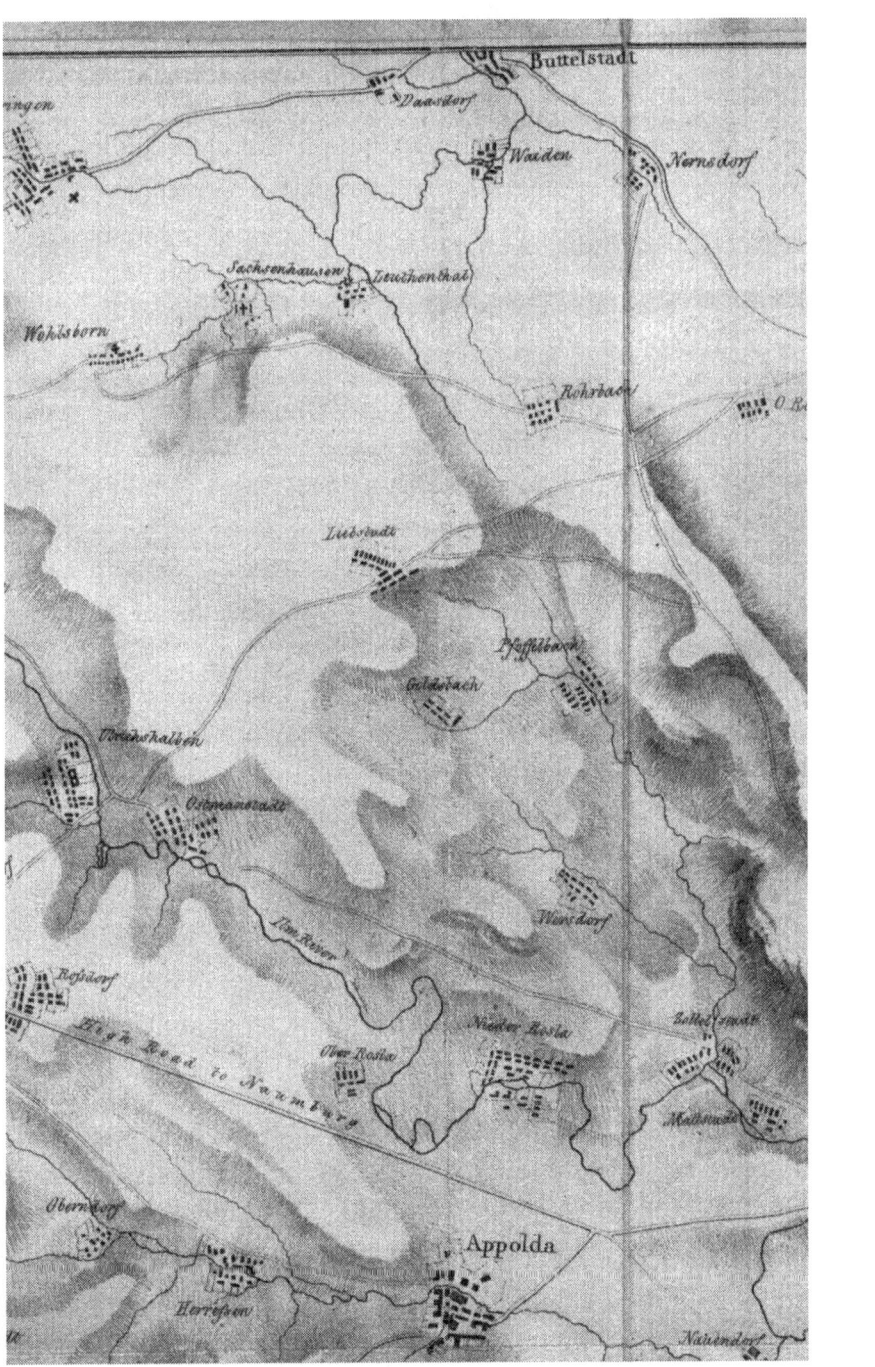

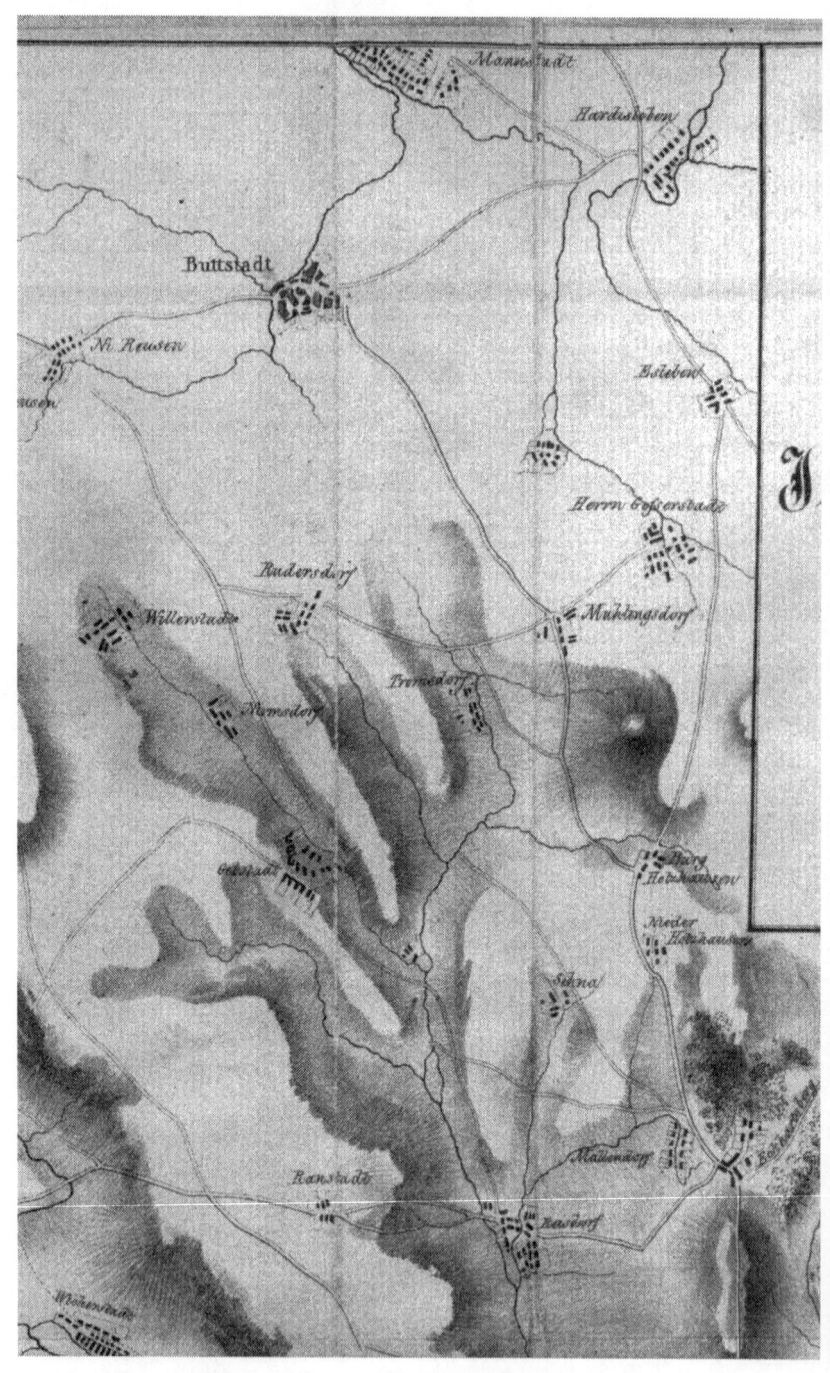

SKETCH
of the COUNTRY between
Jena, Weimar & Naumburg,
in
SAXONY.

Scale of English Miles

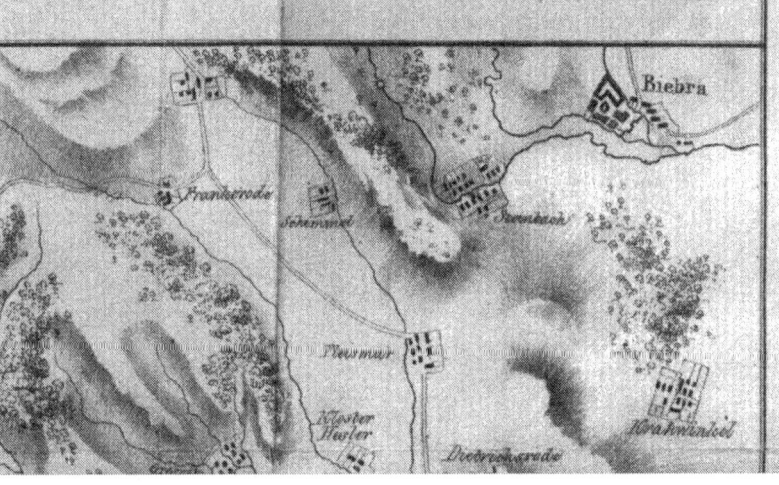

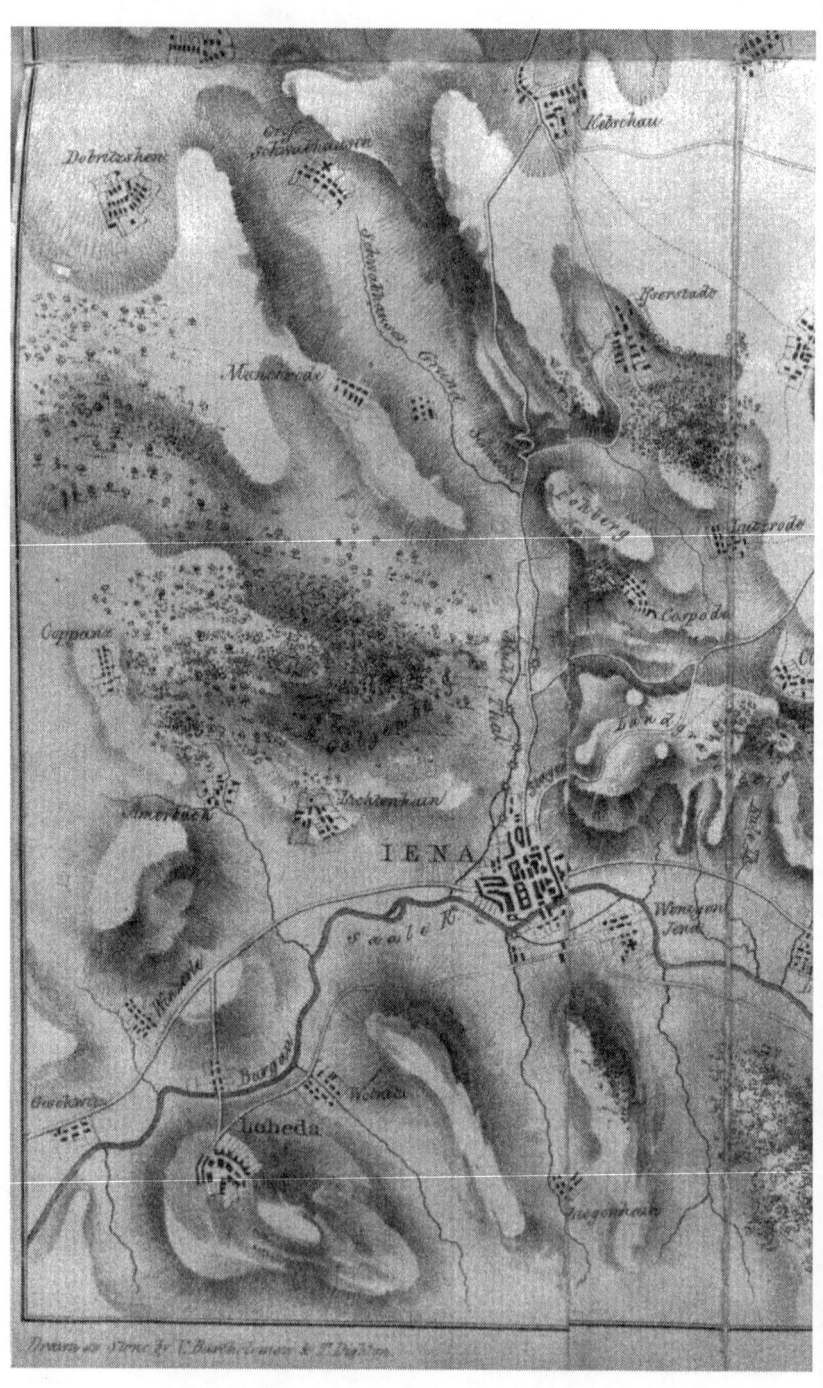

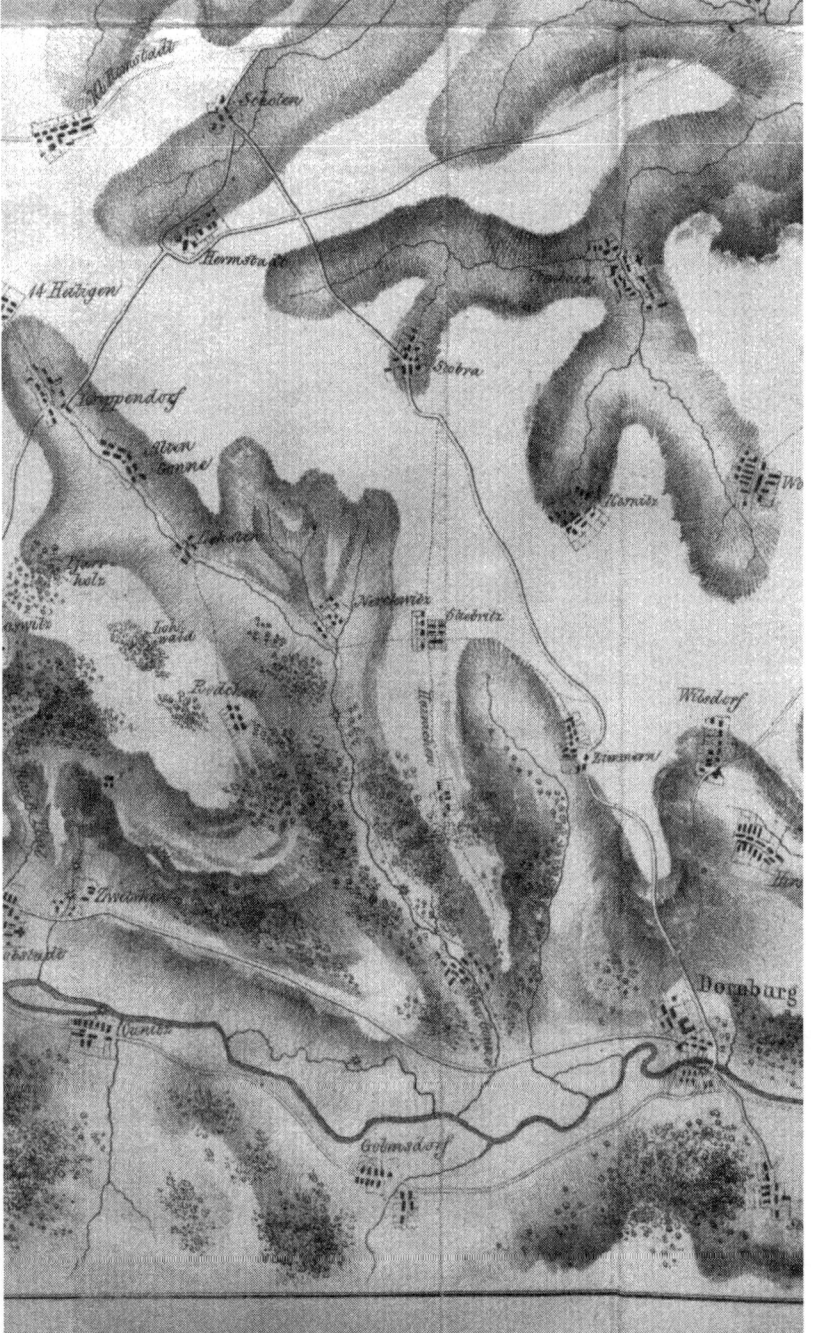

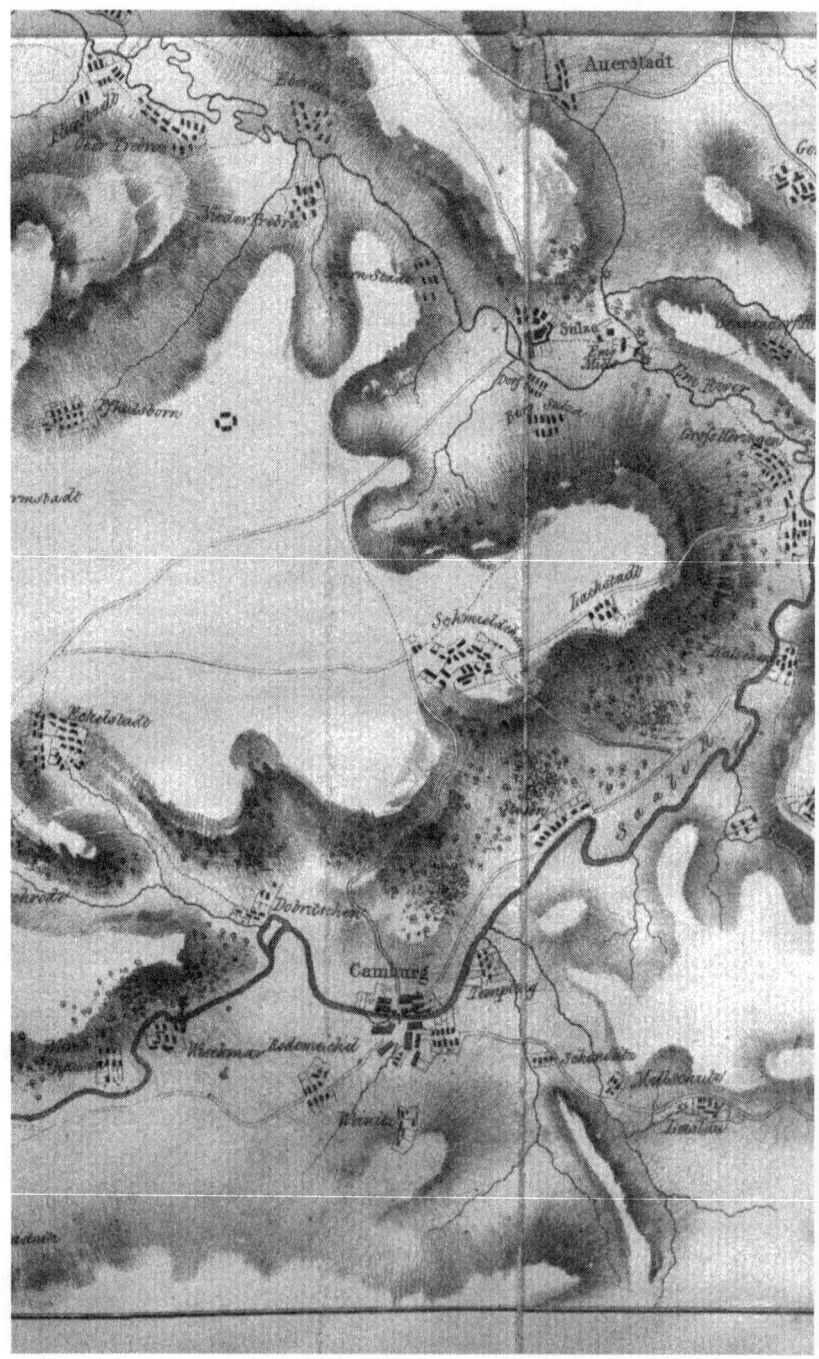

www.ingramcontent.com/pod-product-compliance
Lightning Source LLC
Chambersburg PA
CBHW031156160426
43193CB00008B/387